Jasleen Dhamija h
of textiles, folk art
the Handicrafts Board and for the next seventeen ye
involved in the revival of crafts, and in community development
and women's employment. It was while she was working for the
UN in Iran (1970-77) for the revival of arts and crafts that she
wrote *Living Cultural Traditions of Iran*. From 1978 to 1982
Jasleen headed the Pan-African Centre for Development of Small
Industries and Crafts. Since 1994 she has been working in Central
Asia for the revival of the cutural traditions of the Silk Route.

Jasleen has been the Hill Visiting Professor, University of
Minnesota, Resident Fellow at Canberra School of Art, Creative
Arts Faculty at the University of Wallongong, and Sydney College
of Arts in Australia. She has written over a dozen books on crafts,
textiles and living cultural traditions. During her extensive travels
she has sampled different cuisines, collected innumerable recipes
and improvised them to her taste. She combines her passion for
food with an abiding interest in Ayurveda. For the last ten years
she has concentrated on evolving recipes for healthy eating based
on the Ayurvedic system. *The Joy of Vegetarian Cooking* was
published in April 2000 and created great interest because of her
innovative easy-to-cook healthy recipes.

Cooking
for All Seasons

Jasleen Dhamija

PENGUIN BOOKS

Penguin Books India (P) Ltd., 11 Community Centre, Panchsheel Park, New Delhi 110 017, India
Penguin Books Ltd., 80 Strand, London WC2R 0RL, UK
Penguin Putnam Inc., 375 Hudson Street, New York, NY 10014, USA
Penguin Books Australia Ltd., 250 Camberwell Road, Camberwell, Victoria 3124, Australia
Penguin Books Canada Ltd., 10 Alcorn Avenue, Suite 300, Toronto, Ontario M4V 3B2, Canada
Penguin Books (NZ) Ltd., Cnr Rosedale & Airborne Roads, Albany, Auckland, New Zealand

First published by Penguin Books India 2001

Copyright © Jasleen Dhamija 2001

10 9 8 7 6 5 4 3 2 1

Typeset in Sabon by Mantra Virtual Services, New Delhi

Printed at Chaman Offset Printers, Delhi

For Himman, a gourmet and an aesthete, who encouraged my early efforts at cooking.

Contents

Acknowledgements

I wish to acknowledge the encouragement of all my friends and family when my first cookbook *The Joy of Vegetarian Cooking* came out. It was their appreciation, Mrs Bhicoo Manekshaw's approval and Karthika's enthusiasm that made me put this book together, as I lay immobilized with a broken leg.

I wish to thank Sherna Wadia, a patient, meticulous editor, who has taken so much trouble over the manuscript and put up with my tenacious argumentativeness.

I am grateful to all my friends who were the guinea pigs as I tried out various recipes. I am most grateful to Chotelal, my housekeeper and cook, who has become a vegetarian recently, and had to put up with an array of different meats, fish and sauces. One day he finally did protest. He said, 'After this I am not going to touch barda (beef) and you will have to have separate utensils for it.'

I must thank Babu K.V., who put all my scribbles into a methodical document, and Leela, who waited patiently for him to come home.

Introduction

Cooking for All Seasons is a companion to my first cookbook *The Joy of Vegetarian Cooking.* I do not think of myself as a cook, for I am not able to make the wonderful food that the rest of my family produces. Initially, my interest in food was theoretical. Whenever I was working in a new region or an unfamiliar country, I would taste the local food and learn as much as I could about the culinary history, taboos and traditions of the area. I worked in the fifties and sixties with Kamaladevi Chattopadhyay, that great lady who was responsible for reviving our cultural tradition, and we travelled the length and breadth of India. Though Kamaladevi was a vegetarian and led an austere life at home, when she travelled she loved to taste the local dishes. She would tell our hosts, 'I am vegetarian, but Jasleen is not,' and she would take pleasure in watching me taste the local prawn dishes, especially in the western coastal area from where she came.

It was because of Kamaladevi that I learnt to appreciate different cuisines. Kamaladevi was a Mangalorean and the first cuisine I learnt to really appreciate was the Saraswat Brahmin cuisine, as well as the delicacies made in Mysore for the Dussehra celebrations. In Hyderabad and

Kothakota, I ate Andhra food at the house of Rameshwar and Shanta Rao. In Chettinad, the Chettiar food was rich and quite extraordinary. I tasted rich meat curries, which had a flavour quite distinct from the north Indian meat dishes, and delicately fried crisp neem flowers. In Bengal, I tagged along when Kamaladevi was entertained by Lady Ranu Mukherjee, a great hostess and gourmet. Thus, my palate too was honed and I developed a catholic taste in food. Later, when I began travelling all over the world I was not inhibited about trying all the different ingredients, tastes and flavours.

In India, the strangest food I ate was at a village market in Bastar. I had seen the men and the women of the Maria tribe buy a red chutney doled out on top of fresh green leaves. They ate it with great relish and gusto, smacking their lips and rolling their eyes. I too went to buy my leaf of chutney—it was sharp, sour and syrupy, made of red ants. I learnt that the Maria ate it not only for its tartness but because it was an antidote to gout and joint pains. The tribals never suffered from rheumatism, whereas for the settlers it was a common ailment.

In Africa I tasted delicious crisp-fried caterpillars, crunching them with chilled beer. There were a lot of other local delicacies. For instance, game in Nigeria turned out to be wild rats! The only thing that I could never eat was dog meat, which is a great delicacy in many parts of South-East Asia, for I am a dog lover. But I am not giving recipes for red ant chutney or fried locusts and caterpillars in this book. My recipes are far more sedate than my experiences.

My first cookbook was written at the insistence of Ishwar Sharma, my friend and holistic healer. It was a one-time effort and I quickly returned to my research and writings on living cultural traditions, which has been a lifetime involvement. However, the rather vehement response of my young carnivorous friends made me sit up and think otherwise. I received several angry e-mails and telephone calls, particularly from male friends, calling me a renegade to all those who preferred a carnivorous diet: 'Where are all your lamb, pork, chicken and duck roasts? Where is the gorgeous steak, which we used to feast on—even if it was buffalo meat and we had to lie down on the floor afterwards to allow it to spread out? Where is the fish grilled with fenugreek leaves? Where are all those subtle soups, which could be made for vegetarians and then have meat added to them for those with more robust tastes? What about those Iranian khoreshths with lamb, so fragrant and pleasing to the eye? What about the chicken cooked with apricot, and the subtle use of sour grapes and pomegranate juice?'

I was reminded then of a story told to me by Kumudini Lakhia, the great dancer and choreographer, and also an extraordinary raconteur, about the visit to Oman by Guru Briju Maharaj and his troupe, for a special celebration. Though they had informed everyone well in advance that they were strict vegetarians, no provision was made for giving them vegetarian food. They stayed in the luxurious palace guesthouse and starved. Breakfast was their best meal, for they got tea, fresh and dry fruit, jams, yoghurt and naan, but all the other meals were with meat. Even the salads had chopped eggs sprinkled on top! The only things they could eat during the rest of the day were yoghurt and naan. On their last day, they were told that they were getting a very special meal. Everyone was very excited. After a week of near starvation, they were going to feast.

With great ceremony they were ushered into the hall and there in front of them on a large table was stretched out a whole roasted camel, with the ingredients cascading out of the stomach—a stuffed goat, inside which was a lamb stuffed with a chicken, which had in turn an egg inside it. It had been decorated with herbs, salads and fruits. When Panditji saw this offering, he fainted and had to be carried back to the guesthouse. Luckily, he was leaving the next morning.

Unlike in India, in parts of Central Asia, the Middle East and Africa, the concept of vegetarianism is quite alien. In India, Rajasthani cuisine has something similar to the Omani dish described above: a stuffed lamb with one thing inside the other. The whole is then covered with wet mud and buried underground. Twenty-four hours of slow cooking in its own juices, along with the added herbs and spices, makes it a most delectable dish, ideal for an autumnal night amidst the sand dunes. You can break off chunks of the natural pot, with meat sticking to it, and nibble at it as you sip ayesha, an aromatic drink flavoured with saffron, which is so strong that it can only be consumed in drops from a bird-shaped chuski.

I have also had in Rajasthan khad khargosh—rabbit baked in the earth. The rabbit is cleaned, marinated with herbs, spices, onion, garlic, ginger and green chillies, wrapped in chapatti and cooked underground. The lady who made it refused to part with the recipe. She said, 'This is my khazana (treasure), for which people come even from abroad.' However, this is a thing of the past, for it is illegal to hunt rabbits now.

Being fond of unusual meat preparations myself, I decided that perhaps my friends were right and I should write another cookbook. And this time I would include my meat recipes that are not heavy-handed on spices and oil, and are based on dietary rules for healthy living. After all, most households do eat non-vegetarian food and many of them have both vegetarian and non-vegetarian members in their families. Then again, though the Ayurvedic system believes in a vegetarian diet, the Unani system encourages the consumption of meat for building up strength and for those illnesses which are debilitating. Yakhani, a soupy meat stew, is specially made with trotters for strengthening the system. Eggs eaten raw, or beaten with milk, is given for breakfast to children with persistent coughs in winter. This was certainly the bane of my childhood. Of course, a teaspoon of brandy added to it changed the flavour and made it more palatable. In the Unani way, eating pigeon, for example, is part of the treatment for a stroke. (Pigeon in Egypt has another function. In the rich delta region, the fields are dotted with beautifully constructed mud and brick pigeon-cotes. The pigeon droppings make a very rich fertilizer. At the same time, roasted pigeon is an essential diet for a jaded husband. It is a subtle hint that his performance levels do not match the spouse's ardour.)

Having decided that I would write the book, I started putting together my recipes, only to realize—yet again—that a truly balanced diet has to include both vegetarian and non-vegetarian dishes. I also found that very often my decision to make a certain dish (or not make it) was dependent on what was available in the market at that time. Thus emerged the organizing principle for this book: a collection of recipes that took into account the one important factor that often determines what we eat and when—the natural cycle of the seasons: winter, spring, summer and monsoon.

India is such a vast country that the seasons do not always follow the same pattern. In northern India, where I live, the four seasons are more distinct than in, say, the south where winter has a minimal presence. Spring sets in by February, and we have two balmy months when the gardens are in full bloom. That is when two of our most beautiful festivals, Vasant Panchami, the spring festival, and Holi, the festival of colour, are celebrated. Raag Vasant embodies the beauty of the season, as does the colourful hori, which are the songs sung at Holi. Vasant or spring, though brief, is a wonderful time of the year, when it is still cool and a lot of time can be spent outdoors. No wonder it is associated with Kamdev, the god of love. Everywhere, fresh leaves are sprouting and the fields are covered with yellow mustard flowers.

Traditionally, the yellow colour is associated with Vasant Panchami—yellow clothes, colourful yellow kites, even yellow rice is made with saffron, with chunks of meat added to it for non-vegetarians. In Gujarat, it's time for Makar Sankranti and the great kite festival. In Assam, Bihu is celebrated with offerings of delicacies and woven gamchas to elders.

A few months later, Chait, the first month of summer, is celebrated by the singing of chaiti:

Hathwa lagat kumala gae vai Rama
Juhi kai phulwa
Bela phuli chameli phuli
Aur aam ke ras bahi jave, ho Rama.

(Summer has come when the delicate juhi flower fades with the heat of the body. But then there are compensations, for the fragrant jasmines are blooming and the mangoes are overflowing with juice.)

Summer is ideal for a light cuisine like khoreshth—Iranian dishes of vegetables and chicken or meat. The base of the meal could be a light broth, with cucumber, bottle gourd, zucchini, chicken breast or small mince balls added to the soup. A range of fresh salads, which could tempt the most jaded appetite, can be served.

The rainy season is the most romantic. After the burning, searing heat, when even birds fall from the trees and the earth cracks with dryness, the coming of the monsoon and the greening of the environment are most soothing. When the rain falls on the upturned pipal leaves, the air is cool, but when it stops and the sun shines, it is not only hot, but also extremely humid. The digestive system is very delicate during this season, and the diet has to be light and easy to digest. Stale food and leftovers should be avoided. Fish is also not usually eaten, even in the coastal areas. One reason for this is probably that the fish are spawning at this time.

In most north Indian households salan—a combination of vegetables and meat cooked together—is an important part of the diet. Fish is less common and is generally eaten fried. In the coastal areas, fish is an essential part of the diet, and dried fish is a staple. Fish is much easier on the digestive system than other meat and it also has a number of nutrients which are essential for our well-being.

Winter is the time when you can eat fish without a worry. At other times, I avoid shopping for fish unless I have my icebox with me. In any case, I follow the rule of not eating fish, if I am not next to the sea or the source of the fish, in those months that do not have the letter 'r' in them—May, June, July and August. I do, however, use dried fish for some of my dishes in summer.

Winter

In the northern part of the country, the winter can be short, but quite chilly. From early December to early February, it is pretty cold and it is wonderful to sit by the fireside. I come from the mountains and love the cold weather. When I was in Iran and it snowed, I would put on my pushtin, a sheepskin coat, and go walking in the snow secretly, for I did not want to miss out on the sympathy and the free rides I would get on the icy roads. I really did not know how to drive on them; after all, I learnt to drive in Delhi. My Iranian friends felt very sorry for me when it snowed; they thought that it must be a great hardship for an Indian. People forget what a large country India is and that it has such varying geo-climatic conditions.

Winter in India can be extremely pleasant and one gets to enjoy all kinds of food. Fresh vegetables and delicacies, such as a range of lettuces, celery and asparagus are plentiful, and we can indulge in rich aromatic foods without fear of indigestion. One thing I enjoy serving during the winter season is pork. Many people avoid pork in India because of the unsanitary conditions in which the animals are reared. However, pork is available now from animals raised in farms. The meat has a delectable taste, for it absorbs the aroma of spices and gives a rich flavour. I generally serve pork from October onwards, and there is a rich variety of dishes to be made with it.

But the most enjoyable meal in winter is possibly breakfast. On Sundays, when everyone is at home, breakfast is the occasion for a family feast. Today, dieticians are against a substantial breakfast. If you have a lifestyle where you totter out of bed fifteen minutes before rushing off to work, it is best to have just tea, juice and fruit rather than grab a hasty breakfast and gobble it down. But if you are following a more relaxed routine, enjoy an early morning cup of tea and fresh fruit before your walk or work-out, followed by breakfast before going to work. Have a substantial breakfast, for it is a good meal to start the day with, especially if you are not likely to sit down to another meal until you get back home in the evening.

The great favourite of all north Indian homes is paratha with curd and pickles. Tandoori roti, wrapped in a napkin and kept overnight, and eaten with leftover meat curry is delicious too, as is leftover dal makhani, spread on crisp, freshly toasted brown bread. Then there is nihari, cooked all night and eaten early in the morning. Unfortunately, I have never made nihari, for I am not inclined to spend all night cooking. It is best bought from a good restaurant.

My favourite breakfasts are from the south of the Vindhyas. One of the most delicious is the Kerala speciality, puttu—steamed rice cakes—delicately flavoured with grated coconut and eaten with liquid palm sugar syrup, or steamed bananas, or a hot fish curry. There is also the Mysore dosa, and idli made with vermicelli. These days, ready-to-serve idiappam packets are available off the shelf at any store even in north India. All you've got to do is follow the instructions on the packet and enjoy a tasty breakfast.

Another favourite breakfast is rice soup with chicken, which I had for the first time in Kunming, Sarawak and later in China and all over South-East Asia. It is reminiscent of the kanji eaten as breakfast in south India, though the South-East Asian concept is more elaborate. A large bowl of rice soup with pieces of chicken is served with a range of different sauces, condiments and greens, so that everyone creates their own flavour. Crisply fried fish is also served alongside. I have eaten many versions of this dish and have improvised on it. On a cold winter morning with an icy wind blowing outside, this dish warms you up and makes it possible for you to face the day.

For sheer uninhibited luxury, there was the caviar breakfast that I had once in Copenhagen, at the beautiful hotel I was staying in. When I went down for breakfast, I found that there was only one other person in the breakfast room and he was sitting down to a gourmet repast. I gathered up my courage, walked up to him and said, 'I have always dreamt of a breakfast like this, but lack the courage to have it alone.' The gentleman was quite confounded. He got up and invited me to join him. I was soon ensconced at the table with a glass of champagne before me. Ceremoniously I was offered a blini over which the maître d'hôtel spread melted butter, followed by a dollop of sour cream, and then he served beluga caviar. It was the very best.

I asked my host if I could prepare the next serving the oriental way, and he very cautiously said in a thick accent, 'Ja! Ja! Of course.'

I requested the maître d'hôtel to get us some soft scrambled eggs, a tablespoon of finely chopped onions, black pepper, lemon and Tabasco. I took a warm blini, spread it with melted butter, placed a tablespoon of sour cream in the centre and a surround of scrambled eggs. Over that I sprinkled freshly crushed black pepper and added the caviar on top of the sour cream. A light sprinkling of onions, a squeeze of lemon and a drop or two of Tabasco and I served my host. I drank to his health and waited for him to taste my offering. Tentatively, he tasted it and his face lit up. 'Formidable!' he exclaimed. The feast

ended with a cup of Columbian coffee with cream and a
Havana cigar.

Breakfast

GRILLED GRAPEFRUIT

Serves: 2

1 grapefruit
1 tbsp honey *or* crushed jaggery
A pinch of powdered cinnamon

· Cut grapefruit into half and deseed.

· With a sharp thin curved knife, or a special grapefruit knife, cut around the inside of the skin of the segments.

· Sprinkle with honey or jaggery and cinnamon.

· Place under a hot grill for 5 minutes and serve.

Note: It can also be served chilled without grilling.

P O A C H E D   E G G S

Serves: 1

2 eggs
2 small, wide-mouthed, heatproof glass bowls

- Bring water to boil in a flat pan.
- Break an egg into each bowl and place bowls in boiling water. Cover pan, and bring water to boil again. Continue boiling till eggs are firmly set.
- Remove pan from heat, pass a knife around the eggs, gently slide out on to hot buttered toast and serve immediately.

F R I E D   E G G S

Serves: 1

2 eggs
1 tbsp butter
1 tbsp corn oil

- Remove eggs from refrigerator one hour in advance.
- Place a small non-stick frying pan on heat. Add butter and melt. Swivel pan to coat base. Add oil and heat.
- Break eggs into pan and allow the base to set. Tilt pan and shuffle fat on to eggs with a spatula.
- Lift out eggs with a slotted spatula, drain, place on hot buttered toast and serve immediately.

Cooking for All Seasons

EGGS FRIED WITH BACON

Serves: 1

2 eggs
3 bacon rashers, with fat
1 tbsp butter
1 tomato, cut into half
1 green chilli, slit and seeded

- Remove eggs from refrigerator one hour in advance.

- Place a small non-stick frying pan on heat. Add bacon and sauté in its own fat. Remove from pan while still soft.

- Add butter to pan and melt over heat. Criss-cross bacon rashers across pan and break eggs over them.

- Allow eggs to set. If there are sections that are not cooked, tilt pan and shuffle oil over eggs with a spatula.

- Slide eggs and bacon on to a plate, using a slotted spatula.

- Place tomato into the same pan, with cut sides facing down. Add chilli, fry for a minute and turn over tomato halves.

- Remove pan from heat after a few moments and leave tomato and chilli in the pan for a minute longer.

- Place tomato, right side up, with the green chilli on the side next to the eggs and serve immediately.

SCRAMBLED EGGS WITH VINEGAR — EGYPTIAN STYLE

Serves: 2

4 eggs
Salt and pepper to taste
2 tbsp butter
4 cloves garlic, finely crushed
2 tbsp malt vinegar

- Beat eggs with salt and pepper till frothy.

- Add butter to a non-stick frying pan and melt over low heat. Add garlic and sauté slowly, stirring constantly.

- Whisk up eggs again and pour into pan, spreading them over the surface.

- As eggs begin to set, add vinegar slowly and stir. Keep stirring until eggs have a creamy consistency.

- Serve on crisp toast or with a crisp paratha.

OMELETTE

Serves: 2

There are different ways of making omelettes. There is the classical French method, when the eggs are not beaten too much, and the fluffy omelettes, which are soft in the centre. There are also the thin flat omelettes, which are a favourite in the Middle East. I always like my omelettes soft, and with surprise fillings.

Omelette:

4 eggs
¼ cup milk
½ tsp salt
¼ tsp pepper
½-1 tbsp butter

Filling for cheese omelette (mixed together):

¼ cup grated cheddar cheese
1 tbsp chopped fresh coriander leaves (optional)
Salt to taste

Filling for ham omelette (mixed together):

2 slices ham, finely chopped
5-6 drops Tabasco sauce
Salt to taste

Filling for herb omelette (mixed together):

2 tbsp chopped fresh coriander leaves
2 tbsp chopped fresh mint leaves
2 tbsp chopped spring onions
Salt to taste

- Remove eggs from refrigerator one hour before cooking.

- Beat together eggs, milk, salt and pepper till well blended.

- Melt half the butter in a small non-stick frying pan, swirling it around to coat base and sides of pan.

- When hot and fragrant lower heat and pour in half the egg mixture. Cover pan and cook on low heat for 1-2 minutes till set.

- If there are any soft spots, insert a wooden fork into the area to allow the heat to come through.

- Place half the filling in the centre of the omelette. Fold one side of omelette over the filling and cook for a few moments longer.

- Remove pan from heat, slide omelette directly on to a dinner plate and serve immediately.

- Prepare the second omlette in the same way.

FRIED LIVER

Serves: 4

This is a good winter breakfast dish. It can be served with toast or with paratha. Liver is also given to people suffering from anaemia. I spent my childhood being fed liver, semi-cooked, and even raw, mixed with chopped tomatoes and onions.

250 gms liver
2 tbsp malt vinegar
1 tsp garam masala powder
Salt and pepper to taste
2 tbsp oil
1 onion, sliced in rings (optional)

- Clean and trim liver, removing the transparent skin. Wash and cut into thin slices.

- Mix with vinegar, garam masala, salt and pepper.

- Heat oil in a frying pan, add liver and stir-fry for 2 minutes.

- Sprinkle in 2 teaspoons water, cover pan and cook for 2 minutes.

- Open pan, add onion rings, if used, and mix well. Cover pan, cook for 2 minutes longer and serve.

CHICKEN RICE SOUP

Serves: 6

This makes a real change from the breakfasts usually served in our homes.

1 chicken (about 750 gms), cut into pieces
1½ cups broken rice, cleaned and washed
3-4 lemon grass stalks, tied together in a knot
½ tsp salt

Accompaniments:
½ cup chopped onions, fried crisp
¼ cup finely chopped garlic, fried crisp
Chopped green chillies soaked in malt vinegar
Soya sauce

- Put chicken, rice, lemon grass, salt and 6 cups water in a pan placed on heat. Bring to boil, lower heat and simmer for 20-30 minutes till chicken is tender.

- Remove chicken from pan, shred flesh, discard bones and return flesh to pan. Simmer for 5-7 minutes, adding water if needed. It should have the consistency of a gruel.

- Remove pan from heat and discard lemon grass.

- Place soup on a hot burner in the centre of the table, with the prepared accompaniments on the side.

- You can also serve fried Bombay duck or fried fish fillet, hard-boiled eggs rolled in do'a (p. 241) or fried ham with the soup.

Soups

I often serve chicken rice soup (p. 14) as an improvisation, which makes it a meal in itself. I serve the soup and its condiments as the central dish along with side dishes like fried fish, chicken fingers, crisply fried small herrings or sardines, a platter of herbs etc. Along with it, I serve chilled vodka for those who have a taste for it and wine for the others. It is a wonderful way of spending a couple of hours nibbling, chatting and resting in between bowls of soup.

Winter soups should be rich and hearty. The Iranians whose art of cooking is called ash-pazee—literally meaning soup cooking, and is indicative of the importance of soup in their cuisine—make wonderful, rich and delicious soups. I love their soups and I am sure you will enjoy them too.

A S H - E - A N A R

Pomegranate and Meat Soup

Serves: 6

Ash-e-anar is a very satisfying soup for a cold winter evening.

1 kg mutton, with bone, cut into large pieces
3 tbsp chickpeas (kabuli chana)
1 cup rice, cleaned and washed

1 kg mixture of fresh parsley, mint and leeks, cleaned, washed and
chopped
Salt and pepper to taste
Juice of 2 kg pomegranates (retain 4 tbsp seeds)
2 tbsp lime juice
2 tbsp chopped fresh coriander leaves

Garnish:
1 onion, cut into long, thin slices and fried crisp

- Pressure-cook mutton and chickpeas with 6 cups water for 30 minutes. Remove from heat, cool and open cooker. The meat should drop off the bones.
- Strain soup into a pan, discard bones and return meat and chickpeas to soup. Return soup to heat and bring to boil. Add rice to boiling soup.
- Stir in parsley, mint, leeks, salt and pepper. Cover pan and simmer until all ingredients are cooked.
- Add pomegranate juice and simmer for a further 20 minutes, stirring occasionally.
- Stir in lime juice, adjust seasoning and transfer to a large soup tureen. Mix in coriander leaves and reserved pomegranate seeds and sprinkle fried onions on top. Serve hot.

Variation: **Pomegranate Soup**
To prepare a vegetarian soup as well, cook meat separately with 4 cups water. Cook chickpeas and rice with a vegetable soup cube and 4 cups water. Add greens, salt and pepper and cook for a few minutes. Strain and add half the chickpeas, rice and greens to the meat soup and the rest to the vegetable soup. Follow the recipe through for both soups.

ASH-E-ESPANECH

Spinach and Meatball Soup with Grape Juice

Serves: 6

1 kg spinach, washed, and tender stems and leaves finely chopped
2 leeks, white part only, finely chopped
1 bunch (½ cup) fresh coriander leaves, finely chopped
Salt and pepper to taste
3 tbsp rice flour
Juice extracted from 1 kg sour grapes (green or black) *or* 2 cups
canned grape juice
2 tsp malt vinegar *or* juice of 1½ limes (optional)

Meatballs:

250 gms mince
1 egg, lightly beaten
3 tbsp chopped fresh mint leaves
½ tsp salt
½ tsp pepper

Accompaniments:

1 onion, finely sliced, fried crisp in 1 tsp butter and drained on
kitchen paper
¾ cup walnut kernels, coarsely crushed

· Mix together spinach, leeks and coriander leaves.
  Place in a pan with 3 cups water, salt and pepper.
  Cover pan and cook on medium heat for about 15
  minutes.

· Blend rice flour with ½ cup water. Whisk so that
  there are no lumps, stir into soup and cook for
  another 5 minutes.

- Mix ingredients for meatballs, shape into small balls and drop into soup.
- Bring soup to boil, lower heat, cover pan and simmer for 10 minutes.
- Add grape juice and heat through.
- The soup should be slightly sour. If the grapes are not sour or you are using canned juice, add vinegar or lime juice.
- Serve hot with fried onions and walnuts served in separate bowls, to be added to the soup individually.

Variation: **Spinach Soup with Grape Juice**
This soup can also be made for vegetarians. Cook the greens with a little extra water, remove the soup required for the vegetarians before adding the meatballs and add the proportionate amount of grape juice to both soups.

HAMOD
Sour Chicken Soup
Serves: 6

This soup is Syrian in origin and has become a traditional family soup in Egypt, though each family may prepare it a little differently. I learnt to make it from my friend Elsie, whose grandparents came from Syria while she herself had grown up in Egypt. It is a meal-in-one and a great favourite with my friends.

I have given the recipe with chicken, but you may try it with a beef and marrowbone broth instead or with small, round meatballs that can be seasoned to your taste. The addition of powdered rice to the mince makes very tender 'kofteh'. Leeks are another possible addition. Use only the white part.

1 chicken (about 1 kg)
1 small head of celery
4 cloves garlic, crushed
1 kg bottle gourd (lauki), sliced thick
1 large potato, diced
Juice of 2-3 limes
Salt to taste
½ tsp sugar

Garnish:

¼ tsp dried mint leaves, crushed

· Cut chicken into small pieces.

· Use only half the leaves of the celery, taking them from the inner side. Wash and chop them. Clean stems and chop fine.

- Prepare a soup by covering the chicken completely with cold water and bring to boil. Add garlic, lower heat and simmer until chicken is half cooked.

- Add celery leaves and stems, raise heat and boil for a few minutes.

- Add bottle gourd, potato, lime juice, salt and sugar and cook till all vegetables are tender.

- Remove chicken pieces from soup, discard bones and return chicken to soup.

- Sprinkle dried mint on top and serve.

- This soup is served over plain white rice. A spoonful or two of rice is put into individual soup bowls and the soup, with vegetables and chicken, is poured over the rice.

Variation: **Sour Vegetable Soup**
Increase the quantity of bottle gourd to 1½ kg and use 4 potatoes with ½ cup chopped fresh mint leaves, and omit chicken. Boil celery leaves and garlic in 6 cups water and follow the recipe through, adding fresh mint leaves with the other vegetables.

FISH SOUP

Serves: 4

½ kg fresh fish *or* head, bones, skin and fins
Salt to taste
8 white peppercorns
4 black peppercorns
1 bay leaf (tej patta)
1 carrot, peeled and finely chopped
1 leek, white part only, finely chopped
1 stalk celery, cleaned and finely chopped
1 tbsp butter
2 tbsp flour
2 eggs, lightly beaten till blended
2 tbsp lime juice

Garnish:
1 tbsp finely chopped chives *or* fresh coriander leaves

- Cook fish, with 4½ cups water, salt, peppercorns and bay leaf in a pan for 30 minutes. Strain. Remove fish meat from bones and add to soup. Discard bones.

- Add vegetables to soup and cook until tender.

- Melt butter in a pan, add flour and fry briskly for a few moments. Slowly add one cup of hot soup, mixing well. Add remaining soup and vegetables and simmer for 5-10 minutes.

- Add a little hot soup to eggs and blend. Stir egg mixture into soup. Cook for a few minutes, stirring constantly. Do not allow it to boil, else it will curdle.

- Stir in lime juice and sprinkle over chopped chives or coriander before serving.

Meat, Chicken, Fish & Vegetables

Many people avoid pork in India because of the unsanitary conditions in which the animals are reared. However, now we get pork from animals raised in farms. Pork has a delectable taste, for it absorbs the aroma of the spices and gives a rich flavour. I generally serve pork from the beginning of the winter season—October onwards—and there are really a rich variety of dishes to be made with it.

Winter has a number of vegetables such as carrots, radish, cauliflower, kohlrabi (ganth gobhi), cabbage, bell pepper, green gram (hara chana), green peas, etc. These can be served with any meat dish for a healthy meal.

ROAST PORK

Serves: 6

1 leg of pork (about 3 kg), skin and fat removed

Marinade:

100 gms dried shrimps
2 tbsp whole coriander seeds
2 tbsp cumin seeds
10 dry red chillies
½ tsp fenugreek seeds (methi)
2 walnut-sized balls of tamarind soaked in 1 cup water
½ cup regular soya sauce

¼ cup sweet, thick soya sauce
1 tsp salt

- Dry roast first 5 ingredients of marinade individually on a tava or griddle.

- Extract tamarind pulp and grind together all ingredients for marinade to a smooth paste.

- Make deep gashes in the pork and rub in marinade. Place in the dish in which it will be cooked. Cover with foil and keep in the refrigerator for 1-2 days.

- Remove from refrigerator at least 2 hours before roasting. Open foil and rub marinade, which may be at the bottom of the dish, over the pork. Cover again tightly.

- Place in an oven preheated to 200°C (400°F). Roast for one hour, basting every 15 minutes with a baster or spoon.

- To check if done, pierce meat with a skewer. The juices should come out clear and not pink. It may require anything up to 30 minutes more, depending on the quality of the meat.

- Before serving, remove foil and cook for 10 minutes with the grill on and the door of the oven open.

- If your grill is separate from the oven, just place it under the grill.

- If you do not have a grill, leave it uncovered in the oven for 10 minutes.

- Serve with roast potatoes, stir-fried vegetables and a salad.

SPICY PORK VINDALOO

Hot and Sour Pork Curry

Serves: 4

There are many ways of making vindaloo. It is a hot and sour preparation of pork cooked with spices and the juice of onions, with potatoes added towards the end of the cooking process. It is a dish which originated in Goa, known for its excellent cuisine.

Vindaloo is good served with rice as well as with small crusty buns, called poi in Goa and brun pav in Mumbai.

This is a recipe which my cook Raju, a Tamilian from Kolar Gold Fields, gave me, very reluctantly. He stayed with me in Iran and became quite celebrated for his ready smile and his range of dishes, but I had to stand over him as he made the vindaloo, since his recipes were always very vague and often had some ingredients missing.

You may like to adjust the recipe. I would not use much oil or ghee, for pork has its own fat, and I generally remove the extra fat.

Vindaloo tastes best the day after it has been made. Keep it in the refrigerator overnight. The excess fat will have solidified and will be easy to remove.

1 kg pork, without skin and fat
6 tbsp oil *or* ghee
½ kg (4 large) onions, finely sliced
½ cup malt vinegar
1¼ tsp salt *or* to taste
1¼ tsp sugar
½ kg (3 large) potatoes, peeled, cut into 2-cm cubes and boiled with
1 tsp salt

Ground to a paste:

12 cloves garlic
3½-cm piece fresh ginger
8-10 dry red chillies
1 tsp cumin seeds
6 cloves
3-cm stick cinnamon

- Cut pork into 3-cm cubes.

- Heat 3 tablespoons oil or ghee in a pressure cooker and fry onions till pale yellow and soft.

- Add ground paste and cook for 3 minutes, stirring frequently to prevent it from sticking to pan. Sprinkle in a little water if necessary.

- Add pork and mix well. Stir in vinegar and salt. Bring to boil, add one cup water and cook under pressure for 15 minutes. Cool and open cooker.

- Add sugar and continue cooking till sugar has dissolved.

- Heat 3 tablespoons oil or ghee in a frying pan and fry potatoes, turning them over till golden on all sides. Remove from pan and add to pork.

- Heat altogether for a few minutes before serving with rice or hot crusty rolls.

FRIED PORK CHOPS WITH GRAVY

Serves: 4

4 pork chops (about 800 gms), trimmed of skin and extra fat
2 tbsp oil

Marinade:

1 onion, finely chopped
6 cloves garlic, finely chopped
2 tbsp malt vinegar
2 tbsp soya sauce
½ tsp salt
½ tsp black pepper

- Mix ingredients for marinade, rub into chops and marinate overnight in the refrigerator.

- Remove from refrigerator one hour before cooking.

- Put chops in a pressure cooker with ½ cup water and cook under pressure for 10 minutes.

- Heat oil in a frying pan, remove chops from cooker with a slotted spoon and place into the frying pan. Fry on both sides till browned.

- Pour gravy from the cooker over chops. Cover pan and simmer for 10 minutes. If necessary, add a little water.

- Serve with a salad.

Cooking for All Seasons

KABAB KOUZEH

Armenian Kabab in a Clay Pot

Serves: 4-6

Let me give you a dish made with pork cooked in a sealed pot by the Iranian Armenians. In earlier times, they ate pork, made kalbas—a delicious salami—and also some of the best wine in the Razaiya area. Often the prepared clay pot, called kouzeh, would be sent to the baker to cook in his oven. This was an old local custom.

The original recipe uses only crushed pepper and salt as seasoning. The bay leaves, cardamom, cinnamon and red chillies are my addition.

To prepare clay pot for cooking:

1 medium-sized clay pot with a fitting lid
Enough leaves of any underground vegetable like turnip, radish, carrot, etc. to fill pot
2 tbsp salt
Oil to rub into pot
Dough made with 2 tsp flour and a little water for sealing pot

Kabab:

1 kg boneless mutton, lamb *or* pork, with fat, cut into serving pieces
4 medium-sized onions, chopped
Seeds of 10 black cardamoms, crushed
5-cm stick cinnamon
10 black peppercorns
4 dry red chillies
½ litre (2¼ cups) pomegranate juice
4 bay leaves (tej patta)
Salt and pepper to taste
1 naan or 3 thick khameeri roti (p. 213)

Garnish:

500 gms fresh basil, coriander and mint leaves, washed, cleaned and stems removed, and spring onions, white part only, trimmed

- Wash clay pot and soak in water overnight.

- Wash leaves, dry and chop. Mix in salt. Rub inside of pot with mixture and fill pot with it. Cover, and place on low heat for 10 minutes. Remove from heat and empty it.

- Clean with a dry cloth and rub oil inside. Turn pot upside down and allow it to dry for a couple of hours. It is now ready for cooking.

- Mix meat with onions, cardamom, cinnamon, peppercorns and red chillies in a bowl.

- Place some meat mixture in the pot, pour in some pomegranate juice, cover with one bay leaf and sprinkle in a little salt and pepper. Repeat layering till all ingredients are used.

- Cover pot and seal lid with dough. Place on medium heat and cook for 1-1½ hours or in an oven heated to 180°C (350°F) for 2 hours.

- When ready, place naan or roti on a large serving dish. Remove dough from lid and pour meat over naan or roti.

- Garnish with fresh green herbs on the side and serve with extra naan or crisp chapatti and a salad.

Note: The pot is washed, dried, oiled and kept aside for the next time the dish is to be prepared.

STEAK

Serves: 4

Having given you a number of dishes made with pork, we can now look at some beef and mutton dishes. Beef is not available in India, but we get buffalo meat and that can certainly be made into pot-roasts, steaks, stews, kabab etc.

1 kg fillet of beef, cut into 4 large steaks, with fat trimmed
2 tbsp butter
2 tbsp oil

Marinade:

1 onion, finely chopped
4 cloves garlic, crushed
2 tbsp malt vinegar
Salt and pepper to taste

- Mix ingredients for marinade, rub into steaks and marinate overnight in a refrigerator.

- Remove from refrigerator one hour before cooking.

- Heat butter in a large skillet. When melted add oil and heat through.

- Add steaks and fry on medium heat for 3-4 minutes on each side.

- Serve piping hot with boiled or baked potatoes, a green salad and mustard on the side.

CALDERETA

Meat Stew from the Philippines

Serves: 6

You can use either mutton or beef for this recipe. It is easy to cook and quite delicious.

1 kg mutton *or* beef
2 tbsp oil
10 cloves garlic, chopped
1 large onion, chopped
2 tomatoes, sliced
1 tsp salt
1½ tsp coarsely ground black pepper
1 tbsp hot chilli sauce, like Tabasco sauce
1½ cups beer
3 medium-sized potatoes, quartered
½ cup fresh shelled green peas
2 red bell peppers, pith and seeds removed and sliced into strips
2 green bell peppers, pith and seeds removed and sliced into strips

- Cut meat into 3-cm cubes.
- Heat oil in a pan and brown garlic. Add onion and tomatoes and sauté for 5 minutes.
- Add meat, salt, pepper, chilli sauce and beer. Bring to boil, lower heat and simmer till meat is almost tender. It will take about 30 minutes in a pressure cooker or 1¼ hours otherwise.
- Mix in potatoes and green peas and continue to cook till almost done.
- Add bell peppers and simmer for a few minutes more.
- Serve hot with boiled rice and a salad.

SHALGAM KA SALAN
Curried Mutton with Turnips
Serves: 6

½ kg boneless mutton
1 kg turnips (shalgam)
2 tbsp oil
½ tsp turmeric powder
Salt and pepper to taste

Ground to a fine paste:

2 onions
8 cloves garlic

Ground to a fine paste:

1 tbsp coriander seeds
1½ tbsp cumin seeds
6 cloves
3-cm stick cinnamon
Seeds of 6 black cardamoms
1 tbsp poppy seeds soaked in water for 1 hour

- Cut meat into 4-cm pieces.

- Peel turnips and cut into 3-cm cubes.

- Place turnips in boiling water for one minute and drain. Discard water and set turnips in a colander. This takes away the smell of turnip, which many people don't like.

- Heat oil in a pan and add turnips. Sprinkle with turmeric and fry for 2-3 minutes.

- Remove turnips with a slotted spoon.

- Add meat to pan with onion and garlic paste and stir-fry for 2 minutes.

- Mix in ground masala, salt and pepper and cook stirring until the oil surfaces.

- Add one cup water and transfer to a pressure cooker. Cook for 20 minutes under pressure.

- Cool and transfer back to pan.

- Add turnips and simmer together for 10 minutes.

- Serve with chapatti or rice.

Variation: **Curried Turnips**
Turnips can be made without meat by doubling the quantity of the vegetable. The same quantities of ground masala and paste can be used for making the vegetable. Fry onion and garlic paste, mix in ground masala and fry. Then add fried turnips with water and simmer for 10 minutes.

CELERY WITH LAMB

Serves: 4

This is a very delicately flavoured dish, which is Iranian in origin, and is traditionally cooked with lamb.

½ kg lamb with bone, cut into serving pieces
4 large onions, finely sliced
4 whole dry red chillies
1 large head of celery
2 tbsp olive *or* safflower oil
1 tsp cumin seeds, roasted
2 heaped tsp sugar
1 tsp salt
3 tbsp lime juice

Garnish prepared the day before (optional):
¾ cup curd, beaten till smooth
¼ tsp salt
¼ tsp castor sugar
¼ tsp saffron

- To prepare garnish, mix 3 tablespoons curd with salt, sugar and saffron in a bowl.

- Beat and rub in saffron to release its colour. Add remaining curd and stir well.

- Keep in the refrigerator overnight for the saffron to blend into the curd.

- Pressure-cook lamb with one onion, 2 dry red chillies and one cup water for 20 minutes.

- Strain and discard chillies. Reserve soup.

- Separate celery leaves and wash carefully. Separate the stems from the leaves. Use only half the leaves from the inner stems; the rest can be discarded or used for other dishes.
- Clean stems and cut into 4-cm pieces. Chop leaves.
- Heat oil in a kadhai or deep frying pan. Add 2 red chillies and cumin and fry for ½ minute.
- Add remaining onions and stir-fry until they are translucent and give out an aroma.
- Add celery and meat and stir-fry for 5 minutes.
- Stir in sugar, salt and ½ cup soup. Cook covered for 10 minutes, until celery is cooked but crisp.
- Add lime juice and serve hot.
- Pour the cold garnish over the hot celery and lamb before serving, if desired.

Variation: **Savoury Celery**

This dish can be made without the lamb for vegetarians. Use 2 heads of celery in place of lamb and add water in place of soup to cook the dish.

AAB GOSHT

Meat Stew with Vegetables

Serves: 6

A steam-cooked mutton or lamb stew, aab gosht, is one of the national dishes of Iran. It is a favourite with the rich and the poor and is eaten all over the country. It is also known as dizee from the name of the narrow-necked vessel in which it is normally cooked. It is a meal in itself. The soup is served first and then the meat, beans and vegetables are pounded and served with bread.

The Iranians break pieces of naan, soak it in the soup and eat that with great enjoyment, along with raw onions and fresh herbs.

1 kg mutton *or* lamb, with bone
2 onions, sliced
1 cup dry haricot beans
1 cup chickpeas (kabuli chana)
Dough made from 2 tsp flour and a little water to seal lid of pan
½ kg (3 large) potatoes, peeled and diced
½ kg (6 large) tomatoes, chopped
4 lemu omani (dried lemon)—optional
Salt and pepper to taste

Accompaniments:

Naan
Sliced onions
Mixed green herbs like fresh coriander, parsley, mint, spring onions and basil

- Cut meat into 3-cm cubes and place in a pan with onions, beans, chickpeas and 6 cups water. Bring to boil, cover pan, lower heat to the minimum, seal lid with dough and simmer for 4 hours.

- Open pan and add remaining ingredients. Cover pan, reseal lid and simmer for 30 minutes more.
- You may also place all ingredients in a pressure cooker and cook for 45 minutes.
- Strain soup and set aside.
- Remove bones from meat and discard.
- Pound meat, beans, peas and vegetables together to a fine paste.
- Serve soup hot, with naan, raw onions and herbs. Serve pounded meat with bread after the soup.

BHAJI MA BHEJA
Brain Curry with Spinach
Serves: 6

I love a well-cooked dish of brain. It is however best to make this during winter. With the casual manner in which shops keep their goods refrigerated, one could get a piece which may not be fresh. Bhaji ma bheja is a Parsi dish, which was made by the mother of my very good friend Viloo Mirza.

1 kg spinach *or* 2 packets chopped frozen spinach, defrosted
3 sheep's brains, soaked in water for 30 minutes
3 tbsp oil *or* ghee
2 medium-sized onions, finely sliced
1 tsp turmeric powder
1½ tsp red chilli powder
2 medium-sized tomatoes, finely chopped
3 tbsp finely chopped fresh coriander leaves
1 tsp salt
3 tsp malt vinegar
3 tsp Worcestershire sauce
2 tsp sugar

Ground to a fine paste:
6 cloves garlic
5-cm piece fresh ginger
2 green chillies

- Clean spinach by picking the leaves and retaining the tender stalks. Wash thoroughly and chop fine.
- Remove brains from water and carefully remove the outer membrane, blood vessels and the 2 white

'beads' at the base of each brain. Cut each brain into 3-4 pieces.

- Heat oil in a large pan and fry onions till golden.
- Add ground paste, turmeric, chilli powder, tomatoes and coriander leaves. Stir and cook for 2 minutes.
- Stir in spinach and salt, cover pan and cook for 15 minutes on medium heat.
- Add vinegar, Worcestershire sauce and sugar and cook for one minute.
- Add brains and simmer for a few minutes longer till brains are cooked.
- Serve hot with crisp paratha.

FESENJAN
Chicken or Duck in Pomegranate Sauce
Serves: 6

1 chicken *or* duck (about 1½ kg)
¹₃ cup oil for frying

Sauce:

½ kg walnut kernels, coarsely ground
2 cups pomegranate juice
1 tbsp tomato sauce
¹₃ cup lime juice
¼ cup sugar
1 tsp salt

Garnish:

2 tbsp pomegranate seeds
2 tbsp finely chopped fresh coriander leaves

- Clean and cut chicken or duck into serving pieces.

- Reserve one tablespoon oil and heat remaining oil in a pan. Add chicken or duck and brown well. Add one cup water and simmer until done. Set aside.

- Sauté walnuts in reserved oil on low heat for 5 minutes. Add pomegranate juice, simmer for 5 minutes, stir in remaining ingredients and simmer till thick and sauce-like.

- Add chicken or duck and simmer for 15 minutes. Place chicken or duck in a shallow serving dish and pour over sauce. Sprinkle over pomegranate seeds and coriander leaves and serve with steamed rice and a green salad.

FISH MOLEE

Serves: 4

¾ kg kingfish (seer or surmai), cut into serving pieces through the bone
3 tbsp oil
2 onions, finely chopped
6 cloves garlic, finely crushed
6 green chillies, seeded and cut lengthwise
3-cm piece fresh ginger, cut into thin, long slices
½ tsp turmeric powder
½ tsp garam masala powder
Salt to taste
1 cup thick coconut milk made from 1 fresh coconut

- Wash fish and set in a colander to drain.

- Heat oil in a pan and fry onions till golden.

- Add garlic, chillies and ginger and fry for another minute. Sprinkle in turmeric, stir and fry for a further minute.

- Mix in garam masala powder and salt.

- Pour in coconut milk, lower heat, stir well and simmer for 2 minutes.

- Add fish and simmer on low heat till cooked through. Do not stir after fish is added. Swirl the pan around to mix its contents.

- Serve hot with rice.

MADRAS PRAWN CURRY

Serves: 4

½ kg medium-sized shelled prawns, cleaned and deveined
2 tbsp oil
2 onions, finely chopped
6 cloves garlic, finely crushed
½ tsp turmeric powder
½ tsp coriander powder
½ tsp red chilli powder
½ kg (6 large) tomatoes, blanched, peeled and finely chopped
1 cup unsweetened coconut cream *or* coconut milk made from
1 fresh coconut
Salt to taste
Lime juice to taste

- Wash prawns and set to drain in a colander.
- Heat oil in a pan and fry onions till golden.
- Add garlic and all spices. Sauté for ½ minute.
- Mix in tomatoes and cook till it becomes a thick sauce.
- Stir in coconut cream or milk and salt, and simmer on low heat for 2 minutes.
- Add prawns, cover pan and continue to simmer on low heat for 3-4 minutes.
- Mix in lime juice just before serving.
- Serve hot with rice.

EGG CURRY WITH COCONUT

Serves: 6

Eggs:

8 eggs
Salt to taste
A pinch of ground saffron
4 tbsp ghee, butter *or* oil

Curry:

2 large onions, finely sliced
2 bay leaves (tej patta)
2 cloves garlic, chopped
2 slices fresh ginger
A pinch of powdered cinnamon
A pinch of dry ginger powder (saunth)
1 tbsp curry powder
¼ tsp fenugreek seeds (methi)
½ tsp chilli powder
Salt to taste
1½ cups coconut milk made from 2 fresh coconuts

- Boil eggs for about 10 minutes, until hard-boiled.

- Mix salt and saffron together. Shell eggs and roll them in the mixture.

- Prick eggs all over with a fork, to prevent them from bursting while frying.

- Heat ghee, butter or oil in a pan and fry eggs until golden. Drain and set aside.

- Add onions and bay leaves to pan and fry till onions are brown.

- Add remaining ingredients except eggs and coconut milk. Sauté, stirring constantly till the fat separates.

- Lower heat and add coconut milk and eggs. Cook on low heat for 5 minutes.

- Reheat gently before serving.

- Remove eggs from curry and pour curry into a serving dish. Cut eggs into half and add to curry.

- Serve with rice and a tossed salad.

B U R M E S E   P A P A Y A   S A L A D
Serves: 4

1 raw papaya (about 600 gms), peeled and grated
6 green chillies, seeded and minced
2 medium-sized onions, finely minced
½ cup chopped fresh coriander leaves
Salt and chilli powder to taste
Tamarind juice made from a golf-ball-sized piece of tamarind, 1 tbsp
jaggery and ½ cup water

- Mix all ingredients except tamarind juice in a bowl.

- Pour over tamarind juice, mix again and serve chilled.

LIGHTLY SPICED
VEGETABLE STEW

Serves: 6-8

2 cups stems and very young leaves of bottle gourd (lauki) *or*
pumpkin (kaddu) plant
1 tbsp mustard oil
2 medium-sized potatoes, cubed
1 medium-sized aubergine (baingan), cubed
1 white radish, cut in round slices
1 unpeeled green banana, cut in round slices
Salt and sugar to taste
8-10 green chillies, slit
1 tsp coarsely ground cumin seeds
2 green chillies, coarsely ground
½ tsp cornflour
2 tbsp milk

Ground to a paste with a little water:
¼ tsp turmeric powder
3-cm piece fresh ginger, finely grated
2 tsp coriander seeds

Tempering:
1 tsp ghee
¼ tsp onion seeds (kalaunji)

· Cut stems of bottle gourd or pumpkin plant into
  3-4 cm pieces and coarsely chop leaves.

· Heat oil in a pan. Lightly fry the leaves and stems,
  and remove from oil.

- Add vegetables and ground paste to pan and sauté for 5 minutes. Stir in one cup water, cover pan and cook for 5 minutes.

- Return fried leaves and stems to pan and stir them in gently with salt and sugar. Cover pan and cook for 5 minutes. Do not overcook.

- Add slit green chillies and a little water if necessary, and simmer till vegetables are done and there is still quite a lot of light gravy.

- In a separate pan, heat ghee for tempering. Add onion seeds and stir-fry till they stop spluttering. Pour into vegetables and bring to boil. Lower heat and simmer for a few minutes.

- Stir in coarsely ground cumin seeds and green chillies. Simmer for 5 minutes further.

- Mix cornflour and milk together and pour over vegetables. Check for seasoning and add salt if needed. Stir and simmer for 5 minutes longer.

- Remove from heat and serve with rice.

Note: The important part in cooking this dish is to ensure that the vegetables cook through, but do not disintegrate. If they become a mish-mash, they will neither look good nor taste good.

SHIMLA MIRCH BHARWA
Potato-filled Bell Peppers

Serves: 6

6 large bell peppers
3 tbsp corn oil

Filling:

4 potatoes, boiled, peeled and mashed
2 spring onions, finely chopped
1 green chilli, finely chopped
2 tbsp chopped coriander leaves
1 tsp dried pomegranate seeds (anardana), crushed
½ tsp salt

- Wash bell peppers and blanch in boiling water for one minute to soften. Drain and cool. Slit carefully, without separating them into 2 pieces. Gently remove seeds and set aside.

- Mix all ingredients for filling and stuff into bell peppers.

- Heat oil in a kadhai or wok and add bell peppers. Gently fry on all sides.

- Serve hot.

Cooking for All Seasons

GANTH GOBHI TARIDAR
Curried Kohlrabi

Serves: 6

1 kg kohlrabi (ganth gobhi), with leaves
3 tbsp mustard oil
2 dry red chillies
¼ tsp powdered asafoetida (hing)
½ tsp turmeric powder
1 tbsp aniseed (saunf) crushed
1 tsp salt

- Wash kohlrabi and snip off the leaves. Cut off thick stems from leaves and retain leaves whole.

- Scrape off skin of kohlrabi and cut into 2-cm thick round slices.

- Heat oil in a pan. Remove from heat and add red chillies and asafoetida.

- Return pan to heat, add turmeric, stir for a few seconds and add kohlrabi slices and leaves.

- Stir-fry for one minute and stir in aniseed.

- Pour in 3 cups water and add salt. Stir together and cook on low heat for 25 minutes or till tender. You can also cook it in a pressure cooker for 10 minutes.

- Check that the vegetable is cooked through.

- Serve hot with rice.

MATAR PANEER
Green Peas with Cottage Cheese
Serves: 4

2 cups shelled green peas
2 tbsp oil
½ kg cottage cheese (paneer), cut into 3-cm pieces
2 dry red chillies, broken into pieces
1 tsp turmeric powder
1 tsp cumin seeds
1 onion, finely chopped
1 tsp salt

- Boil green peas for 5 minutes in salted water, drain and set aside.

- Heat oil in a pan and fry paneer. Remove from oil with a slotted spoon, drain and set aside.

- Add red chillies to pan and sauté for a minute.

- Sprinkle in turmeric and cumin seeds. Sauté for a minute further.

- Add onion and fry until light brown.

- Add peas and stir-fry for 3-4 minutes.

- Stir in paneer and salt and cook together for 5 minutes further.

- Serve hot.

MOONG DAL AUR SUA SAAG

Husked Green Beans with Dill

Serves: 6

1 cup husked green beans (moong dal)
4 tbsp oil *or* ghee
2 medium-sized onions, finely sliced
1 green chilli, finely chopped
1½ tsp salt *or* to taste
2 medium-sized tomatoes, blanched, peeled and finely chopped
1 cup chopped fresh dill leaves (sua saag)

Garnish:

2 tbsp chopped fresh coriander leaves

· Wash dal and soak in water for one hour or longer.

· Heat oil or ghee in a pan and fry onions for 3 minutes.

· Add chilli and continue cooking till onion is golden.

· Drain dal, rinse in fresh water and add to pan with salt. Cook for one minute and mix in ½ cup water.

· Layer tomatoes and dill over dal, cover and simmer on low heat for 10 minutes.

· Add ¾ cup water and mix. Bring to boil, lower heat, cover pan and simmer for 10-15 minutes or till dal is cooked but not mushy. The grains should remain whole and separate.

· Pour into a dish and garnish with coriander leaves.

SARSON DA SAAG

Puréed Mustard Greens

Serves: 6

Indian mustard or *Brassica juneca* belongs to the broccoli family. It is considered as the 'plant for long life'. Scientists have now found that it has powerful anti-cancer elements. It has thrice the amount of calcium, potassium and iron compared to other leafy vegetables. They call it 'nature's magnet' as it absorbs minerals. It is no wonder that the Punjabis are so robust, as it is their daily diet throughout winter and spring.

2 kg mustard greens (sarson ka saag)
½ kg spinach
10 cloves garlic, finely chopped
50 gms fresh ginger, finely chopped
¼ cup vanaspati ghee *or* margarine
½ cup cornmeal (makki ka atta)
50 gms fresh ginger, finely slivered
6 green chillies, finely chopped
1½ tsp salt
2 tbsp butter

- Wash mustard greens and spinach separately.

- Separate thick stems of mustard from leaves. Peel stems. Chop leaves and stems of mustard and leaves and tender stems of spinach.

- Place in a pan with garlic, chopped ginger and ¼ cup water and cook covered for 20 minutes on low heat.

- Add half the ghee or margarine and stir with a heavy ladle crushing greens for 10-15 minutes. Set aside.

- Put remaining ghee or margarine in a kadhai or wok. Add cornmeal and stir-fry till golden brown.

- Add slivered ginger and chillies. Stir-fry for 2 minutes and add to the greens.

- Sprinkle in salt and stir with a ladle mixing together. Cook for 10-15 minutes or until fat comes to the surface.

- Before serving heat through, add butter and mix in. Serve piping hot.

- Sarson da saag goes well with curried mutton, or pork, curd and makki ki roti (p. 214), served with melting butter on top.

VEGETABLE CUTLETS

Serves: 6

100 gms carrots, cut into 1-cm cubes
1½ cups shelled green peas
1 tsp salt *or* to taste
½ kg (3 large) potatoes, boiled, peeled and mashed with 1 tsp salt
Oil as required
4 medium-sized onions, finely chopped
½ cup dry breadcrumbs
1 egg, beaten till frothy

- Boil carrots and green peas together with salt, till soft. Mash and add to potatoes. Mash together till smooth.

- Heat 2 teaspoons oil in a pan and fry onions till soft and golden. Remove onions from oil, add to vegetables and mix well.

- Divide mixture into 12-14 portions and shape into oval cutlets 8-9 cm long.

- Put breadcrumbs in a plate and press in each cutlet to coat all sides.

- Pour oil into a frying pan to a depth of one cm and heat till medium-hot.

- Dip each cutlet into egg and fry, turning once, till golden on both sides.

Sweets & Desserts

GAAJAR AUR KHAJOOR MITHAI

Carrot and Date Sweet

Serves: 6

The desi or local Indian carrots are much sweeter and the colour is also more intense than the vilayati or English variety. Always use those.

1 kg local carrots (desi gaajar)
1 cup sugar
1½ tsp corn oil
1 tsp roasted sesame seeds (til)
½ cup crushed jaggery
1½ tsp dry ginger powder (saunth)
1 tsp caraway seeds (shahi jeera)
½ kg seedless dates, chopped

Decoration:
10 almonds, soaked in water, peeled and slivered

· Peel carrots, top and tail them (remove one cm from each end) and cut into 3-cm round slices.

· Cook for 5 minutes in boiling water and drain.

· Place ½ cup water and sugar in a pan, add oil and cook until it achieves a thick pouring consistency.

- Add carrots, sprinkle in sesame seeds and mix well.

- Brush a flat serving platter with oil, so that the carrots don't stick to it and arrange carrots on it.

- Heat jaggery in a kadhai or wok until melted. Mix in ginger powder, caraway seeds and dates. Stir till dates are well mixed in.

- Pour over carrots, sprinkle with almonds and serve. Do not refrigerate.

DRY FRUIT COMPOTE

Serves: 6

½ cup sugar
5-cm stick cinnamon
1 tbsp black peppercorns
10 cloves
2 bay leaves (tej patta)
200 gms dates, seeded and washed
200 gms dried apples, sliced or chopped
200 gms seedless, dried apricots, cut into half
200 gms sultanas (kishmish), stems removed
2 tbsp lime juice
½ cup brandy

- Place a pan on heat with 2 cups water, sugar and all spices. Stir and cook till sugar is dissolved.

- Add dried fruits, one after the other, stirring for a few minutes before adding each ingredient.

- Cook for 5 minutes on high heat, stirring continuously. Lower heat and add lime juice. Cook on very low heat for 10-15 minutes.

- Pour in brandy before serving. You can serve this with ice cream or thick clotted cream.

SPICED RICE PUDDING

Serves: 6

½ cup powdered rice
3 cups full cream milk
½ cup sugar
1 tsp caraway seeds (shahi jeera)
1 tsp fennel seeds (badi saunf)
1 tsp aniseed (saunf)
¼ tsp dry ginger powder (saunth)

Decoration:

1 tsp chopped almonds
1 tbsp chopped pistachio

- Blend powdered rice into a smooth paste with a little milk in a pan. Slowly add remaining milk, and mix well.
- Add sugar and all spices.
- Place pan on heat, bring milk to boil, lower heat and simmer, stirring constantly. Cook for 15-20 minutes until it thickens to the consistency of a thick porridge. Scrape base of pan while stirring so that the mixture does not stick.
- Pour into a bowl and smoothen surface.
- Decorate with alternate lines of almonds and pistachios and serve at room temperature.

RABDI

Cream of Milk

Serves: 4

2 litres full cream milk
½ cup sugar
¼ tsp kewra essence
15 almonds, peeled and slivered

· Put milk into a large, shallow kadhai or wok and bring to boil. Reduce heat and simmer for a few minutes. Add sugar and stir till dissolved.

· Allow cream to form on the top, push it to the side of the kadhai and mix it into the milk. Scrape the base of the pan, so that the milk does not burn.

· Continue the process for 30 minutes, scraping the sides and base and mixing the cream into the milk to allow milk to thicken.

· Remove from heat and stir in kewra essence and almonds.

· Chill and serve.

KHAJOOR AKHROAT LADOO

Date and Walnut Sweet

Makes: 20 plum-sized ladoo

200 gms seedless dates, chopped
200 gms walnut kernels, chopped
Milk if required
2 tbsp castor sugar

- Grind dates and walnuts in a food processor to make a stiff paste. Moisten with a few drops of milk if necessary.
- Shape into 20 balls, roll them in castor sugar and serve with ice cream or by itself.

KHURMANI LADOO

Apricot Sweet

Makes: 10 plum-sized ladoo

200 gms apricots, seeded, chopped and soaked in ¼ cup milk
3 tbsp castor sugar
10 pistachios, peeled

- Grind apricots with 2 tablespoons sugar in a food processor to make a stiff paste.
- Roll into 10 plum-shaped balls and roll them over remaining sugar.
- Place on a platter and put a pistachio on top of each ladoo.

Spring

S pring in India is very brief. It begins with the festival of Vasant and ends with Holi, and lasts about forty days. When I was younger, during this festive period, we would fly kites and go on picnics. The gardens would be in bloom and the fields alive with yellow mustard flowers. The colour yellow dominated the season: we wore yellow clothes, used saffron and turmeric to give a yellow tint to the food—zafrani pulao (pulao with saffron), besan kadhi (curd and gram flour curry, tinged yellow with turmeric) and gaajar methi (carrot and fenugreek). Greens too were abundantly available in spring, with fresh herbs growing in open spaces and gardens. The food was mainly vegetarian except at picnics when the men cooked kabab or meat in a handi, a round-bottomed earthenware pot, buried underground.

We in India are really not oriented to the open air and picnics, except perhaps in the valley of Kashmir. In Iran, picnics are an essential part of life during spring and summer. One of the most memorable picnics I have ever had was in Saqez in Kurdistan Ostan, Iran. It was early summer and the orchards were full of fruit.

I was with a group of young field workers making a socio-economic study of Kurdistan. One Friday, a holiday, we asked our hotel to direct us to a picnic spot. They sent us to an apricot orchard, with a stream flowing through it. We arrived in our jeeps with an improvised picnic, and the local picnickers were amazed to see an Indian woman in a sari. Before we knew it, we were part of a large extended family and were seated on beautiful red carpets with fruits placed in front of us. The matriarch, wearing her traditional dress, sat at the head of the carpet, smiling and smoking a pipe. She had a samovar bubbling in front of her and with great grace and warmth she offered us tea.

Suddenly we heard the piercing note of the surna, an instrument similar to the shehnai, and the echoing and haunting melody of the daf, a rounded drum held in the hand. The traditional musicians who come to picnic spots to play for the picnickers had arrived.

Soon everyone was dancing. The men danced vigorously with the women, who swayed with delicate flowing movements of their hands. Young and old, all danced, and the place was transformed into a joyful Garden of Eden. They tried to teach me, and I too attempted to dance but, as a colleague said, I danced like a piece of frozen sculpture. It is true. I couldn't dance to save my life.

The picnic meal consisted of dolmas—stuffed vine leaves—and naan served with meat freshly roasted on the open fire, which the men busied themselves with. The Iranian picnic generally consists of naan, paneer or cottage cheese and herbs, along with dolmas and fresh mutton cooked at the picnic and made into kababs.

While in Tehran we would drive out every Friday and see people picnicking in any open space, especially where there was a flowing stream. Meat sellers set up temporary stalls and families going on picnics bought meat and charcoal for barbecuing the meat.

My son and I went on simple picnics to our favourite place in the mountains of Tehran known as Haft Hauz, which means seven pools, carrying a naan bought on the way, some cheese and salami and a chocolate. It was our quality time together, spent walking up the mountain and telling each other made-up stories.

I would like to start my section for spring with food for picnics. Picnics should be easy to transport and curried items do not really work out. I generally carry disposable cups, forks, spoons and leaf-plates, but I always have real glasses for nothing tastes good in plastic ones.

The traditional north Indian picnic would have stuffed paratha, vegetables for a salad, hard-boiled eggs, shammi kabab and crisp-fried potatoes. A box of mixed sweets may be brought along with packets of savouries to be served before people settle down to the real business of eating.

Picnic Recipes

SALAD FOR AN INDIAN PICNIC

Carry one piece of each vegetable for 2 persons. Wash, clean and wrap them in a clean towel. Carry salt, pepper and lime along with a large dish of stainless steel.

At the picnic, people can pitch in to make the salad.

ALU SAKRORDH

Crisp-fried Potatoes

Serves: 6

6 large potatoes, boiled and peeled
4 tbsp oil
4 dry red chillies
2 tsp salt
1 tsp whole coriander seeds
1 tsp cumin seeds

- Cut potatoes into medium-sized pieces.

- Put oil into a kadhai or wok (not non-stick) and heat until smoking. Add chillies and stir for a few seconds.

- Add potatoes and sprinkle with salt, coriander and cumin seeds. Stir until potatoes are coated with oil and seeds are well distributed.

- Spread potatoes as widely as possible at the base of the kadhai.

- Allow potatoes to stick to the base. Using a khonchi—a heavy straight metal spatula having a sharp edge—scrape base of pan until all potatoes sticking to the base are removed. Stir together, spread potatoes again and repeat the process 2-3 times until potatoes are golden brown and crisp on all sides.

Note: Do not use a non-stick pan to prepare this dish as the potatoes have to stick to the base of the pan to get crisp and golden brown.

SHAMI KABAB

Spicy Kabab

Serves: 6

⅓ cup oil
2 small onions, minced
4 cloves garlic, minced
1 tsp lime juice

Mixed together:

500 gms finely minced lean mutton
1 tbsp coriander powder
1 tsp fresh ginger paste
½ tsp red chilli powder
½ tsp poppy seeds (khus khus) soaked and ground
1 tsp desiccated coconut
¼ tsp powdered cloves
¼ tsp powdered cinnamon
½ tsp powdered seeds of green cardamoms
2 tbsp roasted gram (bhuné chané), powdered
Salt to taste

- Heat 2 tablespoons oil in a pan and fry onions and garlic till brown. Add mince mixture, stir well and cook slowly for 10-15 minutes.

- Allow to cool and grind or pound into a paste with lime juice. Form into round cutlets.

- Heat 2 tablespoons oil on a griddle and fry a few cutlets at a time, for about 5 minutes on each side, till light brown. Add more oil for each batch.

- They can also be served hot with drinks or as part of a meal.

AN IRANIAN PICNIC

Buy naan from Afghani shops or make khameeri roti (p. 213).

Prepare salad as for the Indian picnic, but carry plenty of small cucumbers for people to peel and enjoy, as well as herbs like fresh mint, coriander, parsley and spring onions.

SEEKH KABAB

Barbecued Mutton

Serves: 6

1½ kg boneless mutton, cut into 3-cm cubes
1 tbsp butter

Grind to a paste for marinade:

3 onions
10 cloves garlic
3 tbsp curd
2 tsp salt
1 tsp black pepper

- Rub marinade into meat and marinate for 24 hours in the refrigerator.
- Carry the meat and butter to the picnic along with charcoal and skewers. If you have a barbecue, carry it with you, otherwise improvise with some bricks.
- Place bits of wood at the base of the barbecue or between the bricks, and lay charcoal on top. Light the wood and start the fire by fanning it.
- Skewer the mutton and when the coal is burning red hot, place the skewers on the fire.
- Brown on all sides, basting with butter, for 10-12 minutes, and serve.

DOLMA BURGHE

Stuffed Vine Leaves

Serves: 6

About 50 vine leaves, fresh or canned
2 tbsp melted butter
6 tbsp lime juice

Stuffing:

⅓ cup rice, washed and soaked in water for 10 minutes
250 gms mince
⅓ cup finely chopped onions
⅓ cup finely chopped fresh coriander leaves
1 tsp salt
½ tsp pepper powder

- If using fresh vine leaves, pick the tender ones. Wash well and boil in water for 10 minutes, till the leaves become pliable. If you are using canned leaves, remove from can, gently wash in cold water and drain.

- Drain rice and mix with remaining ingredients for stuffing in a bowl.

- Place about 20-25 leaves flat on the base of a pressure cooker.

- Put a leaf on a board with the vein side up. Nip off the stem, if any, and near the stem end put a level teaspoon of stuffing. Fold the stem side over the mixture. Fold the sides of the leaf towards the inside to cover the stuffing. Gently roll and place into the cooker. Roll as many as you can—approximately 25 to 28.

- Place a heavy stainless steel plate over the dolmas to weigh them down. Gently pour in 1½ cups hot water and half the lime juice. Close cooker and cook under pressure for 10 minutes.

- Remove from heat and allow to cool. Open cooker and lift out the plate.

- Lift out dolmas with a slotted spoon and place in a dish.

- Mix together melted butter and remaining lime juice. Pour over dolmas just before serving.

- They are delicious, hot or cold.

Soups

FISH STOCK

Makes: 6 cups

Bones, head, tail and skin of fish
1 bay leaf (tej patta)
1 onion, roughly chopped
2 tomatoes, roughly chopped

- Mix all ingredients in a pan with 7 cups water, bring to boil, lower heat and simmer for 30 minutes. Strain.

- Remove flesh from bones and reserve for the soup. Discard the rest.

ESHKANEH SHIRAZI

Curd Soup with Meatballs

Serves: 4

This recipe was given to me by an Iranian friend, Ferangiz Shadman, who was a Namazi from Shiraz. The Namazis are a well-known family that traded with India and China in earlier days.

1 tbsp oil
1 onion, finely minced
1 tsp flour
1 tsp dried mint leaves, crushed
3 cups broth made with 3 bouillon cubes
Salt and pepper to taste
1 cup curd, hung for 2 hours to remove excess water
6 walnuts, crushed

Meatballs:

250 gms mince
1 small onion, finely minced
2 tbsp finely minced fresh coriander leaves
1 egg, lightly beaten
Salt to taste

- Heat oil in a pan and fry onion till golden. It should not brown.

- Lower heat, stir in flour and cook for a few moments, taking care it does not brown.

- Add mint and fry for a couple of seconds. Pour in broth and bring to boil. Add salt and pepper.

- Mix all ingredients for meatballs, shape into small balls and drop into boiling broth.

- Cook for 10 minutes and remove from heat.

- When ready to serve, beat curd with a fork till smooth and pour into soup. Reheat, but do not boil.

- Stir in walnuts and serve.

Variation: **Curd Soup**
This soup can also be made for vegetarians. Use vegetable soup cubes instead of boullion cubes and before adding the meatballs take out the amount of soup needed. Add the meatballs to the remaining soup and then follow the recipe through for both soups.

FISH AND CELERY SOUP—
TWO DISHES IN ONE

Serves: 6

Whole fish is cooked in a fish stock and the soup is served first. The fish can be served afterwards as a separate dish. The fresh celery which is added to the soup changes its flavour, so the two dishes don't taste similar.

3 small fish like seer, salmon or black pomfret (about 250 gms each),
cleaned and gutted, but kept whole
1 lime
Extra salt to rub on fish
Stalks of 1 head of celery, cleaned and washed
6 cups fish stock (p. 70)
¼ cup olive oil
3 large onions, cut into 4 pieces each
4 potatoes, peeled and cut into bite-sized pieces
3 carrots, cut into 1-cm cubes
Salt and pepper to taste
1 cup boiled rice
6 egg yolks
6 tbsp lime juice

Accompaniments:

Lime wedges
Chopped fresh mint leaves

· Wash fish, rub with lime and salt and set aside.

· Roughly chop half the celery and finely chop the rest.

· Pour fish stock into a pan large enough to lay all the fish flat on the base. Bring to boil and add oil. Add all vegetables except finely chopped celery and mix in salt and pepper. Cook for 10 minutes.

· Lower heat and place fish gently on top of vegetables. Cover pan and simmer gently for 15 minutes.

· Remove from heat and with a long slotted spatula transfer fish carefully to a large, round, warm, heat-proof dish.

· Strain soup. Arrange vegetables around fish, sprinkle over one ladle of soup and set it in a warm oven.

· Return soup to heat, add reserved celery and boil for 6 minutes. Stir in rice.

· Blend egg yolks till fluffy and slowly add lime juice while continuing to blend. Gradually add one ladle of soup, mixing it in well and set aside for 5 minutes.

· Reheat soup, remove from heat and slowly blend in half the egg sauce.

· Serve in a soup tureen with lime wedges and a bowl of chopped mint on the side.

· Add remaining sauce to the warm fish and serve after the soup with more lime and mint.

FISH RASAM

Spicy Fish Soup

Serves: 6

250 gms boneless fish
1 tbsp butter *or* ghee
1 onion, finely chopped
2 cloves garlic, finely chopped
1 tbsp coriander seeds, roasted and ground
½ tsp turmeric powder
2 tbsp freshly ground black pepper
½ tbsp fenugreek seeds (methi), roasted and ground
½ tbsp cumin seeds, roasted and ground
Salt to taste
6 cups fish stock (p. 70)
A walnut-sized ball of tamarind soaked in ½ cup water
2 tbsp lime juice

· Wash fish and cut into bite-sized pieces.

· Sauté onion in butter till golden. Add garlic and fry for ½ minute. Sprinkle in spices and salt, and sauté for 2 minutes.

· In the meantime, bring stock to boil. Add ½ cup stock to spices, mix well and transfer to boiling stock.

· Extract tamarind juice and add. Add fish and cook for 10 minutes.

· Add lime juice and serve hot.

Meat, Chicken, Fish & Vegetables

KOFTA KADHI HYDERABADI

Meatballs in Curd Sauce

Serves: 6

Kadhi:

½ cup gram flour (besan)
1 tsp turmeric powder
1 tsp red chilli powder
1 tsp salt
2 cups sour curd, beaten till smooth

Tempering-I:

2 tbsp oil
A pinch of powdered asafoetida (hing)
4 dry red chillies

Meatballs:

250 gms mince
3 tbsp roasted gram (bhuné chané), powdered
1 tbsp fresh ginger paste
½ tsp powdered seeds of green cardamom
½ tsp finely minced green chillies, without seeds
½ tsp salt
½ cup oil

Tempering-II:

2 tbsp butter
1 tsp cumin seeds
1 tsp garam masala powder

- Mix gram flour, turmeric, chilli powder and salt for kadhi. Add one cup curd and mix to a smooth paste. Add remaining curd and mix well. Stir in 3 cups water, ensuring that no lumps are formed.

- Heat oil in a large pan for the first tempering. Add asafoetida and red chillies and stir for ½ minute.

- Add curd mixture and stir for about 15 minutes till mixture thickens. Remove from heat and set aside.

- Mix all ingredients except oil for meatballs. Shape into balls the size of small limes.

- Heat oil in a kadhai or deep frying pan and fry meatballs till brown. Remove from oil, drain, add to curd mixture and simmer for 10 minutes on low heat.

- Before serving, heat through without allowing to boil, and pour into a serving dish.

- Melt butter for the second tempering in a small kadhai or frying pan. When hot, add cumin seeds and brown for ½ minute. Add garam masala and stir together for ½ minute further. Pour over kadhi and serve with rice or khameeri roti (p. 213).

HAAQ AUR GOSHT

Kashmir Greens with Mutton

Serves: 6

Haaq, the everyday vegetable of the Kashmir Valley, is grown on the floating islands, created by the boat dwellers on the lake, as well as on the land. Cooked simply with very little spice it adds flavour to rice and cooked with meat it is food fit for the gods.

½ kg mutton, with bone
1 kg haaq greens
3 tbsp mustard oil
¼ tsp powdered asafoetida (hing)
2 dry red chillies
2 large black cardamoms, powdered
2 tsp salt
2 tbsp aniseed (saunf), crushed

Ground to a paste:
2 medium-sized onions
8 cloves garlic
4 green chillies
6 cloves
1 tsp coriander seeds
2 dry red chillies
2 tsp turmeric powder
1 tsp dry ginger powder (saunth)

· Cut mutton into 2-cm pieces, with bone. Wash and set aside.

· Wash greens well to remove all grit, discard thick stems and chop leaves and tender stems.

- Heat oil in a pressure cooker until it smokes. Lower heat and add asafoetida. Stir for ¼ minute, add whole red chillies and cardamom and stir for ½ minute longer.

- Mix in ground paste and fry for about 5 minutes till oil separates.

- Add mutton and stir-fry till browned. Pour in one cup hot water and salt and stir together. Cook under pressure for 20 minutes.

- Cool and open cooker. Stir in greens and aniseed.

- Close cooker and cook under pressure for 10 minutes longer.

- Cool and open cooker. Check if meat and greens are cooked through.

- Stir together, check for salt and if necessary add ¼ teaspoon more. Cover with a plain lid and simmer without pressure for 5 minutes further.

- Serve hot with boiled rice.

RARDHA GOSHT

Pot-roasted Masala Lamb

Serves: 6

1 kg lamb, cut into 4-cm pieces with bone
4 tbsp oil
1 tsp garam masala powder

Marinade:

2 cups curd
3-cm piece fresh ginger, ground to a paste
10 cloves garlic, finely crushed
1 tbsp coriander powder
1½ tsp turmeric powder
1 tbsp chilli powder
½ tsp sugar
2 tbsp salt

- Mix all ingredients for marinade and rub into lamb. Keep overnight in the refrigerator.

- Remove lamb from the refrigerator at least 3 hours before cooking.

- Lift lamb pieces from marinade and drain, reserving the liquid.

- Heat oil in a pressure cooker, add lamb and stir-fry on low heat, sprinkling in a little water at a time, but never adding too much. The oil will separate and lamb will become brown. It should take 10-12 minutes.

- Add reserved marinade and ¾ cup water and stir well.

- Close cooker and cook under pressure for 20 minutes.

- Set aside cooker till cool. Open cooker and if lamb is not tender add ¼ cup water, stir together and cook under pressure for 5 minutes further.

- If there is any liquid in the cooker, cook uncovered, stirring constantly till the liquid has dried out.

- Serve hot, sprinkling garam masala on top.

CARBANADA CRIOLLA

Meat Stew from Argentina

Serves: 6

A lively, young UN volunteer in Iran used to make this dish for me whenever I visited her. It is a meal in itself.

1 kg mutton *or* rump of veal
½ cup oil
1 large onion, chopped
10 cloves garlic, minced
½ kg (6 large) tomatoes, blanched, peeled and chopped
1 cup chopped fresh parsley
¼ tsp dry oregano
1 bay leaf (tej patta)
Salt and pepper to taste
1 carrot, sliced
1 litre (4½ cups) water *or* bouillon
150 gms butter
4 medium-sized potatoes, peeled and cubed
¼ kg yellow pumpkin (kaddu), peeled and cubed
400 gms rice, cleaned and washed
3 ears of corn, cut into 3-cm pieces *or* 1 can corn (200 gms)
1 cup fresh, shelled green peas

- Cut meat into 3-cm cubes.

- Heat oil in a pressure cooker and sauté onion and garlic till golden.

- Add meat and brown lightly.

- Add tomatoes, parsley, oregano, bay leaf, salt and pepper and simmer on low heat for 3 minutes.

- Add carrot, water or bouillon and half the butter and cook for 30 minutes under pressure.

- Open cooker and add potatoes and pumpkin. Close cooker, but do not put on the pressure valve and cook for 10 minutes.

- Add rice, corn and green peas. Mix well, cover cooker again and continue cooking slowly for about 10 minutes further.

- Make four holes in the stew and put in remaining butter. Cover cooker, place on a griddle so that the rice does not burn and cook for another 5-10 minutes on very low heat. Check the rice, it should be cooked through and tender.

- Serve hot with a green salad.

Note: Add more water or bouillon, as needed. The stew should be thick but have a gravy.

MURGH CHANA
Chicken with Chickpeas
Serves: 6

200 gms chickpeas (kabuli chana), soaked overnight
1 large chicken (about 1½ kg)
3 tbsp oil
2 onions, finely chopped
10 cloves garlic, finely chopped
1 tsp turmeric powder
½ tsp black peppercorns
½ tsp freshly ground black pepper
1 tsp salt
Juice of 3 limes

- Drain chickpeas, wash well and cook under pressure, with enough water to cover, for 15 minutes. Drain and reserve water.

- Cut chicken into serving pieces and set aside.

- Heat oil in a pan and sauté onions till golden. Add garlic and fry for one minute.

- Sprinkle in turmeric, peppercorns and ground pepper and sauté for one minute.

- Add chicken, mix well and sauté for 5 minutes. Mix in salt and chickpeas.

- Stir in 2 cups hot chickpea water, cover pan and cook for 12-15 minutes. Check if chicken and chickpeas are done. If not cook for 3-5 minutes more.

- Mix in lime juice and place on a flat platter. Serve with boiled rice.

PA KHING

Steamed Fish with Fresh Ginger

Serves: 4

This is a delicacy from Laos.

750 gms fresh fish fillets
125 gms fresh young ginger
Juice of 1 lime
2 tbsp oriental peanut oil
1 tbsp oriental sesame oil
1 tbsp nam pla (fish oil)
6 cloves garlic, finely sliced
3 tbsp sesame seeds (til), dry-roasted till golden brown
2 tbsp dark soya sauce
1 large banana leaf *or* aluminium foil
White cotton thread

- Wash fish and remove skin.

- Scrape skin off ginger and slice into very fine slivers, almost like threads.

- Mix ginger with strained lime juice and set aside.

- Heat all 3 oils together in a small pan and fry garlic slowly, till pale gold. Take care not to let it burn. Pour oil and garlic over ginger.

- Mix sesame seeds with ginger-garlic mixture. Add soya sauce and mix well. Sprinkle over fish and set aside.

- Cut banana leaf into 4 pieces, removing the central vein. Pass the pieces over a live flame to soften them. Do not let them burn.

- Divide fish mixture into four parts. Place each in the centre of a banana leaf portion. Fold over one side and overlap with the opposite side. Fold over the adjacent sides to form a square or rectangular parcel. Tie firmly with white cotton thread to hold the parcel in place.

- Place parcels in a colander over boiling water and steam for 15 minutes.

- Untie the thread and serve in the banana leaf, for each person to open the packet and eat the fish.

- *Note:* If the banana leaves sound too complicated or you cannot get any, use foil.

LAHORE KAILASH DI
MACHCHI TAMATARVALI

Crumb-fried Fish in Tomato Gravy

Serves: 2

In the mid-1930s, my father ran Hotel Kailash in Anarkali. The well-known Punjabi artist Sardar Sobha Singh was a starving artist at the time. Father encouraged and helped him by asking him to make paintings of the food for the week.

Everyone loved the fish with tomato gravy. Even I, as a baby, remember the aroma of the fish sauce. We dug up the recipe from father's old books and tried to recreate the childhood memories. Of course, in Lahore, we used river fish, but now I use black pomfret.

1 small black pomfret (about ¾ kg), filleted and skinned
1 lime, cut in half, to rub over fish
⅓ cup dry breadcrumbs
1 egg
Oil *or* ghee as needed

Marinade:

½ tsp turmeric powder
1½ tsp chilli powder
1 tsp ajwain
1 tsp salt *or* to taste
3-4 tsp lime juice

Tomato Gravy:

2 tbsp butter
1 medium-sized onion, finely sliced
10 cloves garlic, crushed

½ kg (3 large) ripe red tomatoes, blanched, peeled and chopped
4 cloves
3-cm stick cinnamon
½ tsp ajwain
1 dry red chilli
1 green chilli, finely chopped
2 tbsp finely chopped fresh mint leaves
1 tsp salt
1 tbsp oil
2 tsp flour
3 tsp brown sugar
3 tbsp malt vinegar

Garnish:

Chopped fresh mint leaves

- Wash fish in cold water and rub with lime to remove the smell.

- Mix ingredients for marinade and rub into fish. Allow to marinate for 30 minutes or longer.

- Spread breadcrumbs in a plate and beat egg until light and frothy.

- Pour oil or ghee into a frying pan to a depth of one cm and heat till it sizzles.

- Dip each fillet into beaten egg to coat completely. Press both sides into breadcrumbs and fry, turning once, till golden. Set aside.

- To make the tomato gravy, pour 2 tablespoons oil from the pan in which the fish was fried with one tablespoon butter in a fresh pan and heat. Add onion and garlic and sauté till brown.

- Add tomatoes, cloves, cinnamon, ajwain, red and green chillies, mint leaves, salt and ½ cup water. Mix well, bring to boil, cover pan, lower heat and simmer for 15-20 minutes till tomatoes are very soft.

- Remove cloves, cinnamon and red chilli and discard. Purée the mixture and rub through a sieve.

- In another pan, heat one tablespoon oil with remaining one tablespoon butter. When butter melts, add flour. Cook for ½ minute then stir in tomato gravy, brown sugar and vinegar. Cook uncovered until gravy thickens a little.

- Add fish fillets to tomato gravy and cook together for 5 minutes.

- Place in a serving dish and sprinkle with fresh mint.

- Serve with rice.

ISSO BAYDUN

Sri Lankan Prawn Curry

Serves: 5

15 large prawns (about 1½ kg)
1 tbsp sliced onions
8 cloves garlic
¼ tsp powdered cinnamon
½ tsp saffron
2 bay leaves (tej patta)
Juice of 1 lime
A pinch of castor sugar
Salt to taste
1 cup coconut milk made from 1 fresh coconut
2 tbsp butter *or* ghee for frying

Ground together with a little water:
1 tsp turmeric powder
1 tsp coriander seeds
1 tsp cumin seeds
10 fenugreek seeds (methi)
8 dry red chillies

· Shell prawns and devein, but retain the tail end. Wash thoroughly and set aside.

· Put all ingredients except prawns, coconut milk and butter or ghee into a pan with one cup water. Bring to boil, lower heat and simmer for 10 minutes.

· In a separate pan, heat butter or ghee and fry prawns for 5 minutes. Add gravy and coconut milk and stir together for a couple of minutes.

· Serve with steamed rice or paratha and a salad.

SHRIMPS IN BUTTER SAUCE

Serves: 4

This is a Trinidadian recipe. Most Trinidadian dishes are seasoned with angostura bitters, since it is the home of this product.

1 kg fresh shrimps, peeled, washed and deveined (if not available use frozen shrimps)
4 tbsp butter
Juice of 2 limes
1 tbsp very finely chopped chives
10 drops angostura bitters
Salt and finely ground black pepper

- Thaw shrimps, if frozen. They must be completely defrosted.

- Heat butter in a pan until melted, but do not allow to burn. Add shrimps and stir continuously over low heat for 5 minutes.

- Stir in remaining ingredients. Adjust seasoning and serve at once.

JHINGA BAND GOBHI BHUJIA

Savoury Prawns and Cabbage with Coconut

Serves: 4

200 gms (about 1 cup) shelled, cleaned and deveined prawns
2 tbsp oil *or* ghee
2 medium-sized onions, finely sliced
½ kg cabbage, finely shredded
4 green chillies, slit down the centre
1½ tsp salt
8 tbsp fresh grated coconut *or* 6 tbsp desiccated coconut
2 tbsp malt vinegar

Ground to a paste:
6 cloves garlic
2-cm piece fresh ginger
4 green chillies

- Wash prawns, drain and set aside.

- Heat oil or ghee in a pan and fry onions for 2 minutes. Blend in ground paste and sauté for one minute.

- Add prawns and when they curl up add cabbage, green chillies and salt. Toss to mix. Mix in coconut, lower heat, cover pan and cook for 5 minutes.

- Sprinkle in vinegar. Toss lightly and cook on medium heat for 5 minutes or till mixture is almost dry.

- Serve hot with chapatti.

Variation: **Savoury Cabbage with Coconut**
Use ½ kg extra cabbage in place of prawns.

JHINGA ALU SALAN

Curried Prawns with Potatoes

Serves: 6-8

This is a simple, quick and very tasty way to prepare prawns.

200 gms (1 cup) shelled prawns, cleaned and deveined
½ kg (5 medium-sized) potatoes
2 tbsp oil
2 onions, finely sliced
12-15 cloves garlic, crushed
3 tsp mustard seeds
1 tsp cumin seeds
6-8 dry red chillies, ground with a little water to make a paste
10-12 curry leaves
2 tsp salt *or* to taste

Garnish:
1 tbsp chopped fresh coriander leaves *or* mint leaves

- Wash and drain prawns and set aside.

- Boil potatoes, peel and cut into round slices.

- Heat oil in a pan and fry onions and garlic till brown. Add mustard and cumin seeds.

- When they start spluttering, add chilli paste and curry leaves and cook on medium heat for 2 minutes. Add a little water, if paste tends to stick to base of pan.

- Add prawns, blend well, stir in one teaspoon salt and one cup water and cook covered, for 3 minutes. With a slotted spoon remove prawns from pan and set aside.

- Add potatoes to pan with one teaspoon salt, mix together, cover pan and cook on low heat for 5 minutes.

- Open pan, stir and return prawns to pan. Stir together. Sprinkle in water, if necessary, and cook covered for 3 minutes.

- Serve hot, garnished with fresh coriander leaves or mint.

BATHUA KA RAITA
Spiced Curd with Greens
Serves: 4

Bathua is readily available during the winter and spring months where other leafy green vegetables like mustard greens are sold.

½ kg bathua
1½ tsp salt
2 cups curd, beaten till smooth
½ tsp red chilli powder

Tempering:

1 tbsp butter
1 tsp caraway seeds (shahi jeera), roasted and powdered·
½ tsp mustard seeds

- Remove stems from greens and wash leaves 2-3 times, removing all grit.

- Chop leaves coarsely, put into a pan with one cup water and one teaspoon salt and cook covered for 10 minutes. Remove from heat, drain and discard water. Squeeze out water from leaves.

- Mix curd, chilli powder and remaining salt together and add to the cooked leaves. Mix together and place in a serving bowl.

- Melt butter in a kadhai or small frying pan, add cumin and mustard seeds and stir. When the mustard begins to splutter, pour contents of pan over curd mixture. It is ready for serving.

MIXED BEAN SALAD

Serves: 6

1 cup French beans, trimmed, boiled and cut into 3-cm pieces
1 cup dry haricot beans, boiled till tender and drained
1 cup dry red kidney beans (rajma), boiled till tender and drained
Lettuce leaves to line salad bowl

Dressing:

⅓ cup malt vinegar
3 tbsp oil
½ tbsp sugar
Salt and pepper to taste
3 tbsp prepared mustard
2 tbsp chopped fresh coriander leaves

- Mix together all beans in a bowl.
- Blend ingredients for dressing and add to beans. Toss gently to coat. Cover and refrigerate. This can be made a day earlier.
- Line a salad bowl with lettuce leaves, pour in beans and serve.

Cooking for All Seasons

RICE SALAD

Serves: 2

1 cup leftover rice
½ cup roast meat *or* chicken, cut into small pieces
1 egg, hard-boiled and chopped
1 onion, finely chopped
1 green chilli, finely chopped
1 green bell pepper, pith and seeds removed and finely chopped
1 carrot, finely chopped

Dressing:

1 tbsp oil
1 tbsp vinegar *or* lime juice
Salt and pepper to taste

· Blend well all ingredients for dressing.

· Mix together all ingredients for salad and stir in dressing. Mix well and serve chilled.

Sweets & Desserts

ZAFRANI MEETHÉ CHAWAL

Sweet Saffron Rice

Serves: 6

1½ cups rice
¼ tsp saffron
1½ cups sugar
3-cm stick cinnamon
Seeds of 6 green cardamoms
½ tsp black peppercorns
4 tbsp unsalted butter
2 tbsp sultanas (kishmish), washed and soaked in water

Decoration:
10 almonds, soaked, peeled and slivered

· Wash rice and cook in 4 cups water until it is firm but not completely done. When crushed between the fingers, it should feel as though it has a grain inside.

· Remove from heat and drain.

· Mix saffron with 2 tablespoons water and rub in a marble mortar with a stone pestle until the strands are completely pulverized, and set aside.

- Place sugar with one cup water and all spices in a pan. Place pan on heat, stir till sugar is dissolved and simmer for 20 minutes.

- Melt butter in another pan and add rice and drained sultanas. Sauté rice till golden, add saffron and mix well.

- Stir in sugar syrup and continue to stir and fry till syrup is absorbed.

- Serve hot, sprinkled with almonds.

SAGO PUDDING

Serves: 6

1 cup sago (sabudana), washed
3 cups milk
¼ cup sugar *or* ¾ cup palm sugar (tardh gurd)
1 tsp caraway seeds (shahi jeera)
4 tbsp rose water
¼ cup petals of Indian rose

Decoration:

2 tbsp peeled and chopped almonds

- Place sago, milk, sugar or palm sugar and caraway seeds in a pan and bring to boil. Lower heat and simmer, stirring for 20 minutes, until it thickens.

- Add rose water and rose petals. Mix together, remove from heat and cover pan. This will make the petals wilt.

- Place in a serving bowl, sprinkle over nuts and serve at room temperature.

SPICED COCONUT CUSTARD

Serves: 6

2 sticks cinnamon, 3-cm each
½ tsp powdered nutmeg
10 cloves
2 cups cream
½ cup palm sugar (tardh gurd), pounded
1 can coconut milk *or* 1 cup thick coconut milk made from 1 fresh
coconut
6 eggs, lightly beaten

- Place one cup water and the spices into a medium-sized pan. Pour in cream. Place on low heat for 5 minutes.

- Remove from heat. Cover pan and let it stand for 5 minutes.

- Add palm sugar and coconut milk and return to low heat. Stir until sugar is completely dissolved. Remove from heat.

- Strain to remove spices. Pour into beaten eggs and combine.

- Pour the mixture into six heatproof bowls. Place bowls in a baking tray with hot water coming halfway up the bowls. Bake for 30 minutes in an oven preheated to 200°C (400°F).

- This custard can be eaten warm, at room temperature or chilled.

GAAJAR KA HALWA

Carrot Sweet

Serves: 4

1 kg local carrots (desi gaajar)
1 litre milk
1 cup sugar
250 gms khoya (dried milk), crushed
½ cup vegetable ghee (vanaspati) *or* margarine
¼ tsp powdered seeds of green cardamom
¼ cup peeled and slivered almonds

- Wash carrots, trim both ends and grate.
- Put carrots in a large, heavy-bottomed pan, add ¼ cup water and cook on medium heat for 10 minutes.
- Add milk and cook uncovered, stirring and scraping the base of the pan, for 30 minutes.
- Add sugar and khoya and mix till sugar dissolves.
- Stir in ghee. The halwa will have thickened by this stage and has to be constantly stirred by scraping the base and sides so that it does not burn. This process will take 20 minutes.
- Mix in cardamom and almonds and remove from heat.
- Serve hot or at room temperature.

Summer

A yurvedic practitioners advise the intake of cooling food and drinks in summer. The seasonal vegetables and fruits are cooling and easily digested. They prevent fermentation of food in the body, which produces toxins. Some foods help get rid of the bacteria from the system. In fact, in extremely hot regions, a great deal of red chillies are used in the food, which serves as an effective way of preventing enteric, as well as fermentation of food. However, the chillies are to be eaten along with ghee and buttermilk, as I found out rather painfully when I was touring Telengana in Andhra Pradesh. I love their hot curries and pickles and had a wonderful time sampling them all. However, being afraid of putting on weight, I did not eat the ghee that they wanted to pour over my rice nor did I take sufficient curd and buttermilk. As a result I had acute acidity and arrived miserable in Hyderabad, where my friends had a good laugh and prepared buttermilk sambar and meat cooked with milk and whole spices to cool my system. I had fragrant khichdi with curd and lime pickle. They also served me a number of cooling drinks until I was back to normal. This was a good lesson: one should always follow the eating habits of the local people and if you want to indulge in food the system is not used to, then do so in moderation.

There are many cooling drinks that can be made at home. The most effective is panna, a drink made from raw mangoes. Traditionally, it was made by burying the raw mango in hot ashes as the morning meal was being cooked on the wood or coal fire. This would slowly cook the raw mango right through. After peeling the skin, the inner pulp would be mixed with cool water and jaggery. It was a must for those going out during the day in north India, as a protection from the hot sun and winds of May and June, which dry the very marrow in the bones. Now there are easier ways of making panna.

India is also home to many sherbets. Legend has it that Allauddin Khilji asked his hakeem to prepare a drink that would cool his liver and spleen. The hakeem soaked almonds in a mixture of milk and water overnight, peeled them the next morning, ground them into a fine paste with cardamom and made it into a cooling sherbet. Thus we got the badam sharbat.

It was Noorjehan who introduced sharbat-e-gulab. One morning, when she was walking in an enclosed garden full of fragrant red Indian roses, laden with dew, she was intoxicated by the fragrance. She asked her cooks to prepare a sherbet with the roses and thus emerged the red coloured gulab sharbat, which later evolved to the famous Roohafza, a cooling drink prepared by the traditional hakeems of Hamdard Dawa Khana, popular even today all over India.

When we were kids, we often heard the vendors cry: 'Kalé pilé falsé badé raseelé falsé'. Falsa or gromia is eaten as a fruit and is also made into a delicious natural pink coloured sweet-and-sour sherbet.

'Jamun badé raseelé Ram' was another song that we heard and we would run out into the street to buy the purple jamun-jujubes, which would colour our lips and our hands and ruin our clothes. There is a way to eat jamun bought from a street seller. He weighs the jamun you buy and puts it into a tin. He sprinkles salt and shakes the tin rhythmically. He then pours out the contents on to a green leaf and offers it to you. The bruised skin of the fruit will have absorbed the salt and you eat the purple jamun, sucking at the seed. You eat carefully, so as not to drop the jamun on your clothes, otherwise it will leave a permanent stain.

Another great delicacy is the khus sharbat, made from vetiver or khus. The green colour and the smell of the khus cools the very core of one's being.

Thandai is another popular summer drink. It is a combination of rose petals, aniseed, almonds, the seeds of melons and cucumber, called char magaz, and other condiments, which are ground into a paste and then mixed with cold milk and sugar. Then there is the special thandai that some sadhus and priests habitually drink, with bhang leaves—fresh cannabis—ground into it. Ordinary mortals like us too have it for special occasions. It is the cheapest way to a trip into space. The Sikh Nihangs dressed in their blue clothes make a delectable thandai with bhang. I used to watch them grinding their bhang in round ceramic bowls, with a lacquered wooden churner with ghungroos or bells on them. They sang as they rhythmically churned their bhang:

Baba teeri gadwi da
Sharbat warga pani
Wey! Pani wey pila dai mitra
Koonja maran tahaian
(Oh father, the sherbet from your churner is sweet. Oh friend, give me that heavenly water for I am like the thirsty water bird.)

When I was working in Baluchistan in the seventies, I visited a Sufi khanegah, which is a monastery-cum-shrine. The Sufis were busy preparing bhang and they called it dughe-wahdat, the drink that leads to the state of being one with the spirit of God.

In parts of north India, particularly Bihar, Sattu is the common man's cooling drink and food. Roasted barley ground into a powder, mixed with water and jaggery and had in the day serves as a meal in itself.

Shikanjveen, made from lime juice and sugar syrup, is had all over India and is not only made at home but sold at every street corner. The Iranian skanjaveen is made from homemade vinegar, which is made from grape juice. They dip lettuce leaves into it and eat them while sipping the skanjaveen.

Lassi, or whipped curd, and buttermilk taken with rock salt and a pinch of roasted cumin powder is another must during the summer. The thin buttermilk, which forms after curd is churned to extract butter, has a taste of its own and is believed to be very good for the digestive system. It is known as takra, food for the gods. In south India the meal ends with thin buttermilk for the less affluent, and curd for the well to do. The delicately flavoured buttermilk, tempered with curry leaves, mustard seeds and ginger, is a cooling drink, to be had during the day or with meals. A jug of thin buttermilk on the dining table as a part of the meal is a common sight all over India. Iran has bottled buttermilk called dugh. They also make an aerated drink with it, which is very popular. Dugh-eh-vahadat, the drink of paradise, was another thing altogether! That one got at the shrines of the pirs or saints, in Baluchistan Sistan.

Today all these drinks are still popular and the commercial vendors have added multiple ingredients to them. Lassi makhani, malai lassi, etc., are now listed in travel guides as local specialities that must be enjoyed. The malai lassi available at Mirza Ismail Road in Jaipur and the Chowk in Jodhpur are popular among locals and tourists alike.

Fresh coconut water served in the coconut itself is a great favourite. Today it is sold all over the country. It is supposed to be excellent for the liver and a preventive for jaundice. It is also part of the diet for a diabetic patient. Some naturopaths believe that some forms of cancer, if caught in the early stages, can be treated with coconut water therapy. Beauticians apply it to remove wrinkles and dark smudges under the eyes. Sugar cane juice crushed from fresh sugar cane with a little ginger, is another delicacy and a cure for jaundice.

Once, on one of the hottest summer days in June, I saw a throng of people at a temple. I was told that it was amla ekadasi, one of the greatest fasts of the year. It was dedicated to amla, the emblic gooseberry or Indian hog plum, which is a jade green tart fruit, considered the purest of all fruits. The day was also celebrated as nirjal ekadasi when people did not even drink water and offered sherbet to those who were not fasting. As this is also the time when mangoes and melons are in plenty, these too were offered to the less fortunate members of society. It is amazing how good health has been absorbed into religion. Amla has the highest vitamin C content of all fruit, and it retains its food value even after it is processed. I was told that traditionally no cereals were eaten on the amla ekadasi. Special non-cereal food was cooked under the amla tree, which was first offered to the tree and then at the temple, with a small water pitcher and a fan. The cooked food offered at the temple was then taken home to be eaten by the family.

There are a number of vegetables which grow in the summer months and are cooling for the system. A good proportion of these should be eaten. The intake of meat should be a quarter of the intake of vegetables and salads. A range of salan—combinations of meat or chicken with vegetables—lightly cooked, without excessive spices, should be eaten by urban dwellers.

Quenchers

FRESH PANNA
Raw Mango Sherbet

Serves: 6

Serve panna through the day. But do give it to children before they leave for school or to anyone going out in the summer heat.

½ kg raw mangoes
½ kg jaggery, crushed
6 black peppercorns
¼ tsp salt
Sugar to taste, if required
1 lime (optional)

- Cut off the stem ends of mangoes and wash thoroughly.
- Slice mangoes with skin and put in a large pressure cooker with 10-12 cups water.
- Add jaggery, peppercorns and salt and mix thoroughly. Cook under pressure for 10 minutes.
- Remove from heat and allow pressure to fall before opening.
- Open cooker and allow to cool.

- Strain through a sieve. Remove peppercorns and discard. Crush mangoes by hand and push through the sieve. Discard skin.

- Taste for sweetness, and if necessary add some sugar and mix.

- If you like a slightly tangy taste, squeeze in lime juice to taste.

- Serve chilled.

RIPE MANGO SHERBET

Serves: 6

At the start of the mango season in north India, the mangoes are sour and not particularly delicious. Yet, we are all dying to eat them. Mango sherbet is the next best thing to satisfy the yearning.

2 kg ripe mangoes
½ kg sugar
1 lime

Decoration:

Sprigs of fresh mint

- Wash and peel mangoes and cut into small pieces. Discard seeds.
- Add 8 cups water and sugar to a pan placed on heat. Cook, stirring occasionally, till sugar dissolves.
- Add mangoes, bring to boil, lower heat and cook for 10 minutes.
- Cool and blend in a food processor.
- Add lime juice and chill.
- Serve chilled with a sprig of mint.
- This drink is served freshly prepared and cannot be stored for any length of time.

SHIKANJVEEN

Lime Juice Syrup

Makes: 750 ml

Juice of ½ kg lime (about 1 cup)
Twice the volume of sugar to the juice
¼ tsp salt
Grated rind of 2 limes

Decoration:

Lime slices
Sprigs of fresh mint

- Dissolve sugar in one cup water in a pan over heat, stirring constantly.
- Add lime juice. As soon as it is about to boil, remove from heat and cool.
- To preserve the juice, squeeze rind through a muslin cloth to produce zest.
- Pour juice into a clean dry bottle. Float ½ teaspoon zest on top of the syrup and refrigerate.
- When opening a bottle, remove zest carefully with a knife. Wipe around the mouth of the bottle with a muslin cloth wrapped around a knife.
- Serve diluted with water or soda, a slice of lime and a sprig of mint.
- It will stay in the refrigerator for a week.

ROSE WATER SHERBET

Makes: 1 litre

2 cups sugar
2 tbsp lime juice
2 tsp powdered red food colour, dissolved in 4 tbsp water
¼ cup rose water

Decoration:

Red *or* pink rose petals

- Mix sugar, lime juice and 1½ cups water in a pan, place on heat and stir till sugar is dissolved. Bring to boil, remove scum, lower heat and simmer for 5 minutes.

- Add colouring to syrup and mix well. Mix in rose water and continue to simmer for 2 minutes.

- Remove from heat, cool and pour into a clean bottle.

- Serve with chilled water and a few rose petals floating on the top.

- This sherbet will last for a week in the refrigerator.

SHAHTOOT SHARBAT

Mulberry Sherbet

Makes: 1½ litres

½ kg large black mulberries (shahtoot)
Sugar equal to volume of juice (about ½ kg)
3 tbsp lime juice

- Rinse mulberries gently in plenty of water.

- Remove stems and purée in a food processor.

- Measure volume of juice and measure an equal volume of sugar.

- Mix sugar and juice in a pan and cook on medium heat, stirring till sugar is dissolved. Bring to boil, remove scum and simmer for 5 minutes.

- Remove from heat and add lime juice.

- Cool and store in the refrigerator. It will stay for one week.

- Serve mixed with ice-cold water.

TAMRA-HINDI SHARBAT

Tamarind Sherbet from Egypt

Makes: 1½ litres

I tasted this sherbet in Egypt where they call our very useful tamarind, tamra-hindi. I loved the sherbet for it reminded me of home, but it had nothing in common with our tamarind chutney or cumin water. The making is very simple.

½ kg good quality tamarind
½ kg sugar *or* 1 kg jaggery
¼ tsp salt
6 black peppercorns

Decoration:

Sprigs of fresh mint

- Mash tamarind and wash thoroughly to remove all grit. Soak in 2 cups hot water for ½ hour. Mix in 3 cups water and soak overnight or for at least 2-3 hours.

- Mix with hand and rub through a sieve, discarding fibres and seeds.

- Mix juice with sugar or jaggery, salt and pepper in a pan. Place pan on heat and cook over low heat, stirring till the sugar or jaggery is dissolved. Simmer for 5 minutes.

- Cool and store in bottles up to one week.

- Mix with iced water and serve with a small sprig of mint on top.

Soups

BELL PEPPER SOUP

Serves: 6

This soup was first made for me by two sisters, who are Tartars and were our hostesses in Osh, Kyrgistan.

6 long, green bell peppers
250 gms mince
1 heaped tbsp rice, cleaned and washed
100 gms fresh coriander *or* mint leaves
1 tsp salt
1 tsp black pepper
Juice of 1 lime

- Cut tops of bell peppers around the stems to make a small opening. Remove seeds and discard.

- Dry-fry mince in a non-stick pan for 10 minutes, until it becomes slightly brown.

- Mix with rice. Reserve 2 tablespoons coriander or mint and mix in the rest with half the salt and pepper.

- Half-fill hollowed bell peppers, allowing room for rice to expand. Place at the bottom of a pan and add 7 cups water, carefully from the side. Add remaining salt, pepper and any leftover mince.

- Bring water to boil, lower heat, cover pan and simmer for 12 minutes. Add lime juice, sprinkle in reserved coriander and serve hot.

Variation: **Cottage Cheese and Bell Pepper Soup**
Replace mince with grated cottage cheese (paneer).

ESHKANEH NARENJ

Tangerine Soup with Meatballs

Serves: 6

When I was researching in Birjand, Iran, I tasted this divine soup and have loved its delicacy. During the day, I worked with a team of field researchers in the remote villages, breaking bread with the kath khoda, the headman of the village, and his family. During the night, I was fed delicacies at the palace of the Alams, who were the khans or chieftains of the area and devoted to Tara Ali Baig, the wife of the ambassador and a well-known social worker, who had introduced me to them. They have a very special cuisine and grow the saffron they use.

1 medium-sized onion, finely chopped
1 tbsp butter
4 cups chicken stock
2 cups tangerine juice, freshly extracted
1 tsp salt
¼ tsp pepper
¼ tsp saffron, soaked in ¼ cup hot water
3 eggs, beaten till well blended
4 tbsp lime juice
2 tbsp fresh mint leaves, finely chopped

Meatballs:

250 gms mince
1 egg, lightly beaten
2 tbsp fresh mint leaves, finely chopped
½ tsp salt
¼ tsp black pepper

Garnish:

- Fry onion in butter in a pan till golden brown and add stock. Simmer for 5 minutes.

- Add tangerine juice, salt and pepper and bring to a rolling boil. Stir in saffron.

- Mix all ingredients for meatballs, shape into balls smaller than walnuts and drop into soup.

- Cover pan and simmer on low heat for 10 minutes.

- Beat eggs again, and add lime juice drop by drop beating all the while.

- Remove soup from heat, add mint and leave it open for a while so that the soup is well below boiling point.

- Slowly add egg sauce, stirring constantly.

- Return to heat and warm through. Do not let it boil, else it will curdle.

- Serve in bowls, garnished with mint sprigs.

Variation: **Tangerine Soup**
Omit meatballs and use vegetable stock or water for a vegetarian soup.

YAKHANI MURGH
Mildly Spiced Chicken Soup
Serves: 6

This is a meal in itself when served with rice or chapatti and a salad.

1 large chicken (about 1½ kg), cut into serving pieces
Salt to taste
3 tbsp crisp-fried flakes of onions

Ground to a paste:
10 black peppercorns
1 onion
6 cloves garlic
3-cm stick cinnamon
2 tsp coriander seeds

Garnish:
2 tbsp fresh coriander leaves, chopped
1 tbsp butter

- Cook chicken, masala paste and salt with 8 cups water in a pressure cooker for 20 minutes.

- Open cooker, mix well and simmer for 10 minutes without pressure.

- Strain soup, discard chicken bones and serve soup and chicken separately.

- Garnish the soup with half the chopped coriander leaves if desired. It is best eaten by soaking pieces of bread or naan into it.

- Mix fried onions with the chicken and serve hot, garnished with melted butter and coriander leaves.

CUCUMBER AND CHICKEN SOUP

Serves: 6

3 cucumbers, 20 cm each
50 gms fresh coriander leaves, chopped
3 lemon grass stalks, tied together in a knot
1 tsp salt
2 tbsp lime juice

Ground together for stuffing:
3 chicken breasts, boiled and roughly chopped
50 gms fresh coriander leaves, chopped
½ tsp salt

- Peel cucumbers and discard bitter ones. Slice off both ends, and reserve slices. Remove seeds from inside and discard.

- Stuff cucumbers with ground chicken. Close both ends with reserved slices, using wooden toothpicks.

- Place cucumbers flat in a pan with 7 cups water, coriander, salt, lemon grass and any leftover stuffing. Cover pan and cook on low heat for 15 minutes.

- Remove from heat, discard lemon grass and add lime juice.

- Remove cucumbers from soup, cut each into 4 pieces, place 2 pieces in each bowl, add soup and serve hot.

Variation: **Cucumber and Cottage Cheese Soup**
It can be made into a vegetarian soup by using grated cottage cheese (paneer) in place of chicken.

CHILLED BOTTLE GOURD
AND CURD SOUP

Serves: 6

¼ kg bottle gourd (lauki), washed, scraped and grated
2 cups curd, whisked with 1 cup water
1 onion, finely chopped
¼ tsp red chilli powder (optional)
1½ tbsp fresh mint leaves, chopped
20 sultanas (kishmish), washed and soaked in water
½ tsp salt

- Place enough water to cover bottle gourd in a pan and bring to boil. Add bottle gourd and boil for 2 minutes. Remove from heat and drain.

- Mix bottle gourd with curd, onion, chilli powder, if used, and mint.

- Drain sultanas, add to soup and refrigerate.

- Serve chilled, adding salt just before serving.

H E R B   S O U P

Serves: 6

2 tbsp butter
1 onion, finely chopped
2 medium-sized potatoes, peeled and roughly chopped
1 litre (4½ cups) chicken stock *or* 2 bouillon cubes dissolved in 1 litre
water
Salt and pepper to taste
1 cup chopped fresh mint leaves
1 cup chopped fresh parsley leaves
1 cup coarsely chopped spring onions
1 cup chopped fresh coriander leaves
½-1 cup milk to dilute soup

- Melt butter and cook onion until soft. Add potatoes and sauté for 2 minutes.

- Add stock and simmer until potatoes are tender.

- Add salt, pepper and herbs and simmer for a few minutes until fairly soft, do not overcook, as you want the soup to have a fresh green colour.

- Remove from heat. Cool and blend to a smooth purée in a food processor. Adjust seasoning.

- To serve, reheat with as much milk as you like. This soup can be really thick or moderately thick.

Note: You can vary the herbs by replacing mint with basil, dill or tulsi. I however prefer a generous amount of mint for the best flavour. Use vegetable soup cubes or a vegetable stock instead of the chicken stock to make a pure vegetarian soup.

Salads

CUCUMBER SALAD — MOSCOW STYLE

Serves: 4

2 large cucumbers

Dressing:

¼ tsp salt
½ tbsp lime juice
2 tbsp oil
¼ tsp black pepper
A pinch of red chilli powder
½ cup fresh *or* sour cream

Garnish:

2 hard-boiled eggs, chopped
2 tbsp chopped chives

- Peel cucumbers, discard bitter ones, score them lengthwise and place in iced water for 20 minutes.

- Mix salt, lime juice, oil, black pepper and chilli powder and blend in cream.

- Drain and dry cucumbers just before serving, slice finely and arrange in a salad bowl.

- Pour over dressing, sprinkle with hard-boiled eggs and chives and serve immediately.

SESAME AND GREEN BEAN SALAD

Serves: 6

500 gms French beans *or* sheet beans (sem phalli), trimmed
2 tbsp sesame seeds (til), toasted till golden brown

Dressing:

2 tbsp soya sauce
1 tbsp oriental sesame oil
1 tbsp minced fresh ginger
Salt to taste

- Boil salted water in a pan and add beans.
- When the water boils again, reduce heat and simmer for 5 minutes, until beans are tender but crisp.
- Cool under cold water and drain.
- Mix ingredients for dressing in a bowl. Add beans, mix well and toss gently with half the sesame seeds.
- Pour into a salad bowl and sprinkle over remaining sesame seeds.
- Refrigerate and serve cold.

CRUDITÉ BASKET WITH THREE DIPS

Serves: 10

Vegetable Crudités (The basket can be of any vegetables in season):

1 head cauliflower
1 cup broccoli, cut into 5-7 cm pieces without tough stems
½ cup snow peas
3 carrots, peeled and cut into thin, long slices
2 large red bell peppers, cut into thin, long slices
2 large yellow bell peppers, cut into thin, long slices
2 large green bell peppers, cut into thin, long slices
2 zucchini, cut into thin, long slices

Mixed together and refrigerated for honey-mustard dip:

½ cup Dijon mustard
¼ cup honey
1 tbsp soya sauce
1 tbsp minced spring onion
2 tsp minced fresh ginger
1 tsp salt

Mixed together for Parmesan dip:

1 cup mayonnaise
2 tbsp grated Parmesan cheese
1 tbsp lime juice
½ tsp fresh coarsely ground black pepper
Salt to taste

Whisked with a wire whisk and refrigerated for sour cream and chive dip:

1 cup sour cream
1 tbsp finely chopped chives

¼ tsp salt
A pinch of red chilli powder

- Boil salted water, add cauliflower and cook till tender but crisp. Drain, run under cold water, drain again and keep aside.
- Using the same water, cook all vegetables individually in the same way.
- Keep them cool in the refrigerator.
- Arrange them in a basket lined with foil just before serving and serve along with the dips.

SPINACH AND CHEESE SALAD

Serves: 6

1 packet vegetable soup powder
2 cups curd, beaten till smooth
½ cup mayonnaise
Salt to taste
2 cups grated cheddar cheese
1 kg spinach, well washed, chopped, steamed and drained

- Blend soup powder, curd, mayonnaise and salt. Stir in cheese and add spinach.
- Cover and chill for 2 hours.
- Serve with dry toast or crisp naan.

POTATO AND EGG SALAD

Serves: 6

700 gms (7 medium-sized) potatoes, boiled in their jackets
8 eggs, hard-boiled and peeled
½ cup vinaigrette dressing (p. 233)
Tabasco sauce as required
1 onion, finely chopped
Salt and pepper to taste
1 tsp capers
½ cup mayonnaise
1 bunch lettuce leaves, shredded

- Peel and cut potatoes while still hot, into bite-sized pieces and place in a dish.

- Chop 5 eggs and add to potatoes.

- Mix vinaigrette dressing with one teaspoon Tabasco sauce and onion. While potatoes are still warm, mix in dressing and set aside.

- Cut remaining 3 eggs into half, lengthwise, and scoop out yolks.

- Chop yolks and add salt, pepper and capers. Mix well, then mix in 2 tablespoons mayonnaise.

- Fill mixture into egg whites and place a drop of Tabasco sauce on top of each.

- Arrange lettuce leaves along the base and sides of a salad bowl so that they come to the lip of the bowl. Fill bowl with potato salad and place eggs on top.

SWEET AND SOUR SUMMER SALAD

Serves: 6

1 cup sliced celery
1 cup sliced apples
1 cup sliced cucumbers
Salt and pepper to taste
2 tbsp orange juice
Lettuce leaves to line platter, washed and dried
2 tomatoes, sliced and sprinkled with salt to taste
200 gms cottage cheese (paneer), diced and sprinkled with salt to taste
½ cup mayonnaise

- Mix celery, apples, cucumbers, salt, pepper and orange juice.
- Arrange lettuce leaves in a flat platter. Place salad in the centre.
- Arrange cottage cheese and tomatoes around it.
- Spoon mayonnaise on top before serving.

COLD CHICKEN SALAD

Serves: 6

1 roasted chicken (about 1 kg)
½ cup red wine
1 tbsp soya sauce
1 tsp chilli sauce
½ tsp dry ginger powder (saunth)
Salt to taste
¼ cup finely chopped carrots
¼ cup fresh shelled green peas
¼ cup finely chopped French beans
¾ cup mayonnaise

- Remove all fatty skin from chicken, debone and cut into small, thin strips.

- Place chicken in a flat dish, pour red wine over it to cover completely and set aside for 2 hours.

- Mix soya sauce, chilli sauce and ginger powder. Stir in a little salt, if needed, and mix into chicken. Place in the refrigerator for 1½ hours until chilled.

- Bring a pan of salted water to boil. Add carrots and bring to boil again. Add green peas and when it comes to boil again add French beans. Remove from heat as soon as the water comes to boil. Drain and cool vegetables under running cold water. Drain again.

- Mix mayonnaise with vegetables and place in the refrigerator for ½-¾ hour.

- Mix chicken and vegetables and serve with a green salad, hot bread rolls and butter.

CHICKEN AND ALMOND SALAD

Serves: 6-8

1 tbsp unflavoured gelatine
1 cup mayonnaise
1 cup thick cream, whipped
½ tsp salt
1½ cups cooked, diced chicken
¾ cup almonds, soaked, peeled, toasted and chopped
¾ cup seedless green grapes, halved

To serve:

Shredded lettuce leaves

- Soften gelatine in ¼ cup cold water and dissolve over hot water. Cool slightly. Combine with mayonnaise, whipped cream and salt.

- Fold in remaining ingredients. Spoon into a mould and chill till firm.

- Arrange lettuce in a salad dish and unmould salad over it.

Note: This is an excellent dish for a buffet in summer.

SUMMER HARLEQUIN SALAD

Serves: 6

5 tsp unflavoured gelatine
¾ litre (3⅓ cups) bouillon made with 4 cubes
1 cup white wine
Salt, pepper and sugar to taste
2 tbsp malt vinegar
500 gms boneless, roasted chicken, cut into bite-sized pieces
3 tomatoes, cubed into bite-sized pieces
100 gms mushrooms, sliced and sautéed in 1 tbsp oil
1 cup finely chopped fresh parsley *or* coriander leaves
20 pickled onions, chopped if large, else left whole

Garnish:

Sprigs of fresh parsley *or* coriander leaves

- Dissolve gelatine according to directions on the packet.

- Place bouillon, wine, salt, pepper, sugar and vinegar in a pan and warm gently over low heat. Remove from heat, add gelatine and mix well.

- Pour just enough mixture into a mould to thinly coat base, and let it cool.

- Mix chicken, tomatoes, mushrooms and parsley or coriander.

- Arrange pickled onions in mould, then fill with meat mixture and pour remaining bouillon mixture over it.

- Chill well, unmould on to a dish, and serve garnished with parsley or coriander.

VIETNAMESE SALAD

Serves: 6

1 small roasted chicken, deboned and cut into juliennes
1 tsp minced garlic
1 kg white radish, washed and very finely sliced
1 kg cucumbers, peeled and very finely sliced
2 tsp salt
200 gms carrots, peeled and very finely sliced
1 onion, finely sliced
2 tsp oil
1 bunch lettuce leaves, shredded
½ cup chopped fresh mint leaves
½ cup cleaned and chopped celery stalks
Extra lime juice for sprinkling over salad (optional)

Marinade:

2 tsp castor sugar
2 tbsp malt vinegar

Dressing:

2 tbsp soya sauce
1 heaped tbsp castor sugar
Juice of 2 limes
1 tbsp minced garlic
1 tsp red chilli powder
1 tsp salt
1 tbsp malt vinegar

Garnish:

¼ cup almonds, soaked, peeled, toasted and crushed

- Mix chicken with garlic and refrigerate till ready to use.

- Sprinkle radish and cucumbers individually with one teaspoon salt each and allow to stand for 30 minutes.

- Squeeze water out with your hands, then put into a towel to squeeze out all remaining water.

- Mix ingredients for marinade and marinate radish for 45 minutes.

- Add carrots and cucumbers to radish and set aside for 15 minutes more.

- Drain vegetables, mix in onion and chicken and place in a salad bowl. Add oil and toss. Mix in shredded lettuce, mint leaves and celery.

- Mix ingredients well for dressing, sprinkle over salad and toss gently again.

- Extra lime juice may be sprinkled over the top if desired.

- Garnish with almonds, chill and serve.

SALADE NICOISE

Serves: 6

2 large firm, ripe tomatoes, sliced
2 green bell peppers, deseeded and cut into thin strips
1 cup French beans, cut and boiled
1 onion, finely chopped
150 gms (1 can) tuna
1 tbsp capers
2 hard-boiled eggs, chopped

Beaten together for dressing:
10 drops Tabasco sauce
2 tbsp lime juice
3 tbsp olive oil
Salt, pepper and mustard powder to taste

- Mix all vegetables together.
- Drain tuna, mash and add to vegetables with capers.
- Add chopped eggs.
- Pour dressing over salad and mix gently.
- Refrigerate for one hour and serve.

AVOCADO PURÉE WITH TUNA

Serves: 6

1 bunch lettuce
3 ripe avocados
1 onion, finely chopped
150 gms (1 can) tuna in oil
1 tsp salt
1 tbsp olive oil
1 tbsp capers
2 tbsp lime juice
10 drops Tabasco sauce
6 black olives

- Wash lettuce leaves, dry them and arrange in a flat tray.

- Cut avocados in half. Discard stone and remove flesh, taking care to not break the skin.

- Mash avocado flesh with a fork.

- Drain tuna from oil and flake flesh finely, with a fork.

- Mix all ingredients except olives and lettuce.

- Adjust seasoning and fill avocado shells with mixture. Smoothen top and put an olive on top of each avocado half.

- Place on the lettuce-covered tray and serve.

Meat, Chicken, Fish & Vegetables

KEEMA GAAJAR METHI
Carrot and Dried Fenugreek with Mince

Serves: 6

2 tbsp oil
2 whole dry red chillies
200 gms mince
4 tbsp dried fenugreek leaves (kasuri methi), soaked in 1 cup water
1 kg carrots, peeled and cut into thin, round slices
1 tsp salt
½ tsp red chilli powder (optional)
1 heaped tsp dry mango powder (amchur)

- Heat oil in a kadhai or deep frying pan until it begins to smoke. Add whole red chillies and stir for less than ½ minute.

- Add mince and stir-fry for 10 minutes, sprinkling with water as needed.

- Squeeze out water from fenugreek leaves and add. Mix in carrots, salt and remaining spices and stir briskly for 2 minutes until well mixed.

- Sprinkle in ¼ cup water, lower heat and cook covered for 10 minutes, stirring periodically.

- Open pan and stir-fry on medium heat until the moisture is dried and the fenugreek looks crisp.

- Serve hot with chapatti, curd and any chutney of your choice.

Variation: **Gaajar Methi (Carrot and Dried Fenugreek)**
Use 1½ kg carrots and 8 tablespoons dried fenugreek and omit the mince. Add the vegetables to the sautéed chillies and continue as given.

THAI SPICY MINCE WITH MINT LEAVES

Serves: 4

1½ cups mince
2 tbsp chopped onion
3 cloves garlic
1 tsp nam pla (fish oil)
1 tsp salt
2 tbsp lime juice
1 tsp coriander powder, freshly ground
1 tsp red chilli powder
1 tbsp chopped spring onion

Garnish:

10 fresh mint leaves

- Brown mince in a pan without oil, until it is dry and the pink colour is gone. Place in a mixing bowl.

- Wrap onion and garlic in a piece of foil. Cook on a live flame until almost burnt. Unwrap and pound it. Add to mince.

- Season mince with nam pla, salt, lime juice, coriander powder, chilli powder and spring onion.

- Spoon into a serving plate, top with mint leaves and serve.

DOLMA KALAM

Stuffed Cabbage Leaves

Serves: 6

1 cabbage (¾-1 kg)
1 tsp butter, for greasing baking dish
1 cup tomato sauce

Stuffing:

250 gms mince
½ cup rice, washed and soaked in water
2 onions, finely chopped
1 cup finely chopped fresh mint leaves
2 tbsp cumin seeds, roasted
½ tsp red chilli powder
1 tsp salt

- Bring a large pan of water to boil. Cut off top of cabbage to expose inner leaves. Hold cabbage by its stem and plunge into water for 5 minutes. Remove from water using a skimmer or a metal colander. Cool and pluck out as many of the inner leaves as you can easily.

- Repeat until you have 12-14 leaves.

- Cut large leaves into half and remove the thick central vein. Retain the smaller ones whole.

- Blanch leaves in boiling, salted water until they are pliable.

- Drain and dry with a clean towel and set aside.

- Mix together ingredients for stuffing and divide mixture into 12-14 portions according to the number of dolmas you are going to make.

- Select a leaf and place the stuffing $\frac{1}{3}$ of the way from one end of the leaf. Spread it along the width leaving 1½ cm on each side.

- Fold over upper end of leaf to cover stuffing and fold in the sides to contain it.

- Gently roll leaf and use a toothpick to hold it together.

- Place dolmas in a buttered baking dish, pour over tomato sauce and spread it out evenly. Cover dish with foil.

- Bake for 20 minutes in a moderate oven at 200°C (400°F).

- Remove foil, bake for another 5 minutes and serve.

KARELA KEEMA BHARWÉ
Bitter Gourd Stuffed with Mince
Serves: 4

During the summer and the monsoons, a meal should start with a bitter vegetable. This improves appetite, helps digestion and prevents acidity.

8 (about ½ kg) bitter gourds (karela)
1 tsp salt
2 tbsp oil

Marinade:

1½ cups curd, beaten till smooth
1 tsp red chilli powder
½ tsp turmeric powder

Stuffing:

2 tbsp oil
2 large onions, grated
6 cloves garlic, ground
2-cm piece fresh ginger, ground
250 gms mince
Tamarind pulp made with a lime-sized ball of tamarind and 2 tbsp water
½ tsp salt

· Scrape bitter gourds, removing rough outer skin. Slit lengthwise and remove seeds. Reserve skin and seeds for karela-ka-chilka bhuna (p. 157).

· Place bitter gourds in a pan with salt, cover with cold water and bring to boil. Boil for 1-2 minutes, drain and squeeze out thoroughly to remove the bitter juice.

· Mix ingredients for marinade, rub over bitter gourds and allow to marinate for one hour.

· Heat oil for stuffing and fry onions till pale golden.

· Add garlic and ginger and sauté for one minute.

· Add mince and stir together. Sauté for 3 minutes.

· Stir in ½ cup water, cover pan and cook on low heat for 5-7 minutes.

· Remove from heat, add tamarind paste and salt and mix well.

· Remove bitter gourds from marinade and stuff with the mince mixture. Tie with white cotton thread to retain stuffing.

· Heat 2 tablespoons oil in a frying pan and fry bitter gourds, turning on all sides till brown.

· Mix leftover marinade with ¼ cup water and pour over bitter gourds.

· Continue to cook on low heat for 2-3 minutes.

· Serve hot with plain paratha along with any other dishes.

KEEMA AUR BHARTHA KABAB

Mince and Aubergine Rolls

Serves: 6

1 kg aubergines (baingan)
2 tbsp oil
½ kg mince
1 onion, finely chopped
¼ cup chopped fresh mint leaves
1 tsp salt
1 tsp black pepper powder
Powdered seeds of 10 green cardamoms
2 eggs
½ cup breadcrumbs

· Coat aubergines with a little oil and roast over a live flame until the skin is burnt. Place in a tray kept at an angle to drain liquid.

· Remove skin, cut off the stem ends and discard. Mash flesh with a fork.

· Mix mince with aubergines and remaining ingredients except eggs, oil and breadcrumbs.

· Beat eggs and mix into mince and aubergine mixture. Shape mixture into 8-cm long rolls and gently roll in breadcrumbs spread in a plate.

· Place rolls in a long, well-oiled baking dish.

· Put into an oven preheated to 200°C (400° F) and bake for 12-15 minutes.

· Serve with a salad.

KHORESHTH-E-BADEMJAN

Aubergine with Lamb

Serves: 6

½ kg lamb
6 small tender aubergines (baingan)
Salt as required
3 tbsp chopped onion
⅓ cup oil
1 tbsp tomato purée
3 tomatoes, sliced
3 tbsp ab ghoreh (juice of sour green grapes) *or* 2 tbsp malt vinegar

- Cut lamb into 3-cm cubes.

- Peel aubergines in strips, lengthwise, leaving a 'cap' at the stem end. Make one-cm slits on opposite sides, along the length of the aubergines. Sprinkle with salt and allow to stand for one hour in a dish kept at a slant, to drain the water.

- Sauté onions in 3 tablespoons oil till golden, add lamb and sauté till browned. Stir in tomato purée and cook for a minute. Add tomatoes and one teaspoon salt. Continue cooking for 1-2 minutes.

- Stir in enough water to cover meat. Cover pan and simmer for one hour over low heat, or pressure-cook for 30 minutes.

- Fry aubergines in remaining oil until browned on all sides. Add to meat and simmer on low heat for 5-6 minutes.

- Add grape juice or vinegar, 15 minutes before serving and serve hot with steamed rice.

AMBAVALA GOSHT

Lamb with Sweet Mango Sauce

Serves: 4

½ kg boneless lamb
4 tbsp oil *or* ghee
4 dry red chillies
2 medium-sized onions, finely sliced
1½ tsp salt *or* to taste
½ kg jaggery, crumbled or cut into small pieces
¼ kg pearl *or* button onions, peeled and kept whole
4 fresh ripe mangoes, peeled and cut into 4-6 slices each

Ground to a paste:

6 cloves garlic
2-cm piece fresh ginger

Tempering:

1 tbsp butter
10 curry leaves
6 black peppercorns
½ tsp mustard seeds

- Cut meat into 3-cm cubes and set aside.
- Heat oil or ghee in a pan, add chillies and sliced onions and fry till onions are golden.
- Add garlic-ginger paste and cook for 2 minutes.
- Add meat and brown. Stir in 2 cups water and salt and cook in a pressure cooker for 30 minutes, till meat is tender.
- In another pan place jaggery with 2 cups water.

- Bring to boil, lower heat and simmer covered, till jaggery is dissolved.

- Add pearl onions and when they are almost cooked, add mangoes. Continue cooking till onions and mangoes are soft.

- Just before serving, reheat meat and mango mixtures separately. Place meat in a serving dish and pour mango mixture over it.

- Melt butter for tempering in a small frying pan. Add curry leaves and peppercorns, sauté for one minute and add mustard. When it begins to splutter, pour contents of pan over meat and mango and serve with rice, a vegetable dish and a salad.

TINDAI KA SALAN

Squash and Lamb Curry

Serves: 6

½ kg boneless lamb
1 kg Indian squash (tinda), peeled and quartered
2 tbsp oil
1 tsp turmeric powder
Salt and pepper to taste

Ground to a paste:

2 onions
8 cloves garlic

Masala dry roasted and ground together:
1 tbsp coriander seeds
1½ tbsp cumin seeds
6 cloves
3-cm stick cinnamon
Seeds of 6 black cardamoms

- Cut meat into 4-cm cubes.

- Place squash in boiling water for one minute. Drain and put into a colander.

- Heat oil in a pressure cooker. Add turmeric and squash and fry for 3 minutes. Remove from pan and set aside. Fry meat and onion and garlic paste in pan for 2 minutes.

- Add dry masala powder and continue to fry till masala is cooked and the oil surfaces. Add ½ cup water and pressure-cook for 20 minutes. Add squash, simmer for 5 minutes and serve with rice.

KADDU KA SALAN

Curried Meat with Pumpkin

Serves: 4

½ kg boneless mutton *or* beef, very finely sliced
½ cup oil
2 whole dry red chillies
1 tsp salt
½ kg yellow pumpkin (kaddu), peeled and finely sliced

Marinade:

2 tbsp soya sauce
1 tbsp malt vinegar
1 tbsp cornflour
1 tsp sugar

- Combine ingredients for marinade, mix into meat and marinate for 24 hours in the refrigerator. Remove meat from refrigerator 2 hours before cooking.

- Pour oil into a pan and heat until it smokes. Add chillies and fry for a moment.

- Add meat and ½ teaspoon salt, and stir-fry on high heat until meat turns light brown. Remove meat from pan, leaving the oil in it.

- Add pumpkin and ½ teaspoon salt and cook for 3 minutes without lowering heat.

- Return meat to pan, stir gently and cook for one minute further. It is ready to serve.

- Serve with chapatti.

MUTTON WITH DRUMSTICKS

Serves: 4

400 gms mutton *or* lamb
8 drumsticks, peeled
2 tbsp oil *or* ghee
1 large onion, finely sliced
2 green chillies, kept whole
1¾ tsp salt
350 gms (2 large) potatoes, peeled and cut into 4-cm pieces
1 cup coconut milk from 1 cup grated fresh coconut

Ground to a paste:

6 cloves garlic
2-cm piece fresh ginger

- Cut meat into 4-cm cubes, rub with garlic-ginger paste and marinate for at least one hour.

- Cut drumsticks into 4-5 pieces each, tie into bundles and boil in 2 cups water until almost cooked. Drain.

- Heat oil in a pressure cooker and fry onion till golden. Add meat and cook on high heat till water from meat has dried.

- Mix in chillies, ¾ teaspoon salt and 2 cups water. Pressure-cook for 20 minutes until meat is tender.

- Add potatoes and one teaspoon salt and simmer uncovered till potatoes are cooked. Add drumsticks and coconut milk and cook over low heat for 10 minutes till gravy has reduced and thickened slightly.

- Serve piping hot with rice.

CHICKEN WITH APRICOTS

Serves: 4

1 chicken (about 1 kg)
10 dried, seedless apricots
3 tbsp butter
4 whole dry red chillies
1 onion, finely sliced
¼ tsp saffron soaked in 2 tbsp hot water
Salt to taste

- Cut chicken into serving pieces and set aside.

- Soak apricots in ¼ cup water.

- Place butter in a pan over heat and melt. Add chillies and onion and sauté till onion is translucent.

- Add chicken and sauté for 5 minutes.

- Stir in saffron with the soaking water and fry for another 3 minutes.

- Mix in apricots with the soaking water and salt.

- Simmer, stirring for 10-15 minutes until chicken is tender.

- Serve with rice, a vegetable dish and a salad.

FRENCH BEANS WITH CHICKEN AND TOMATOES

Serves: 6

2 tbsp butter
250 gms boneless chicken, chopped
6 cloves garlic, finely chopped
500 gms French beans, strung and cut into 3-cm pieces
½ tsp caraway seeds (shahi jeera), roasted and powdered
500 gms (6 large) tomatoes, blanched, peeled and chopped
¼ tsp powdered allspice (kabab cheeni)
¼ cup chopped fresh coriander leaves
1 tsp salt
2 tbsp lime juice
¼ tsp red chilli powder

- Melt butter in a kadhai or wok and sauté chicken for 5 minutes. Add garlic and sauté for ½ minute. Add beans and caraway seeds and sauté for 2 minutes.

- Place tomatoes on top, sprinkle in allspice, coriander and salt. Pour in ¼ cup hot water gently from the side. Cover pan tightly, lower heat and simmer for 10-12 minutes. Check if beans and chicken are cooked. If necessary, add a little water and cook until tender but firm.

- Open pan and add lime juice. Cook for 2 minutes without lid, if too watery. It should be moist but all ingredients should be firm, not mushy.

- This dish can be served hot or cold.

MURGH PALAK METHI TARIDAR

Chicken Curry with Fenugreek and Spinach

Serves: 6

1 kg spinach
½ kg fresh fenugreek leaves (methi)
Salt as required
1 chicken (about 750 gms), cut into serving pieces
4 tbsp ghee *or* oil

Ground to a smooth paste:
2 onions, roughly chopped
10 cloves garlic
1 tsp turmeric powder
1 tsp cumin powder
1 tsp coriander powder
¼ tsp fenugreek seeds (methi), roasted and powdered
1 tsp poppy seeds (khus khus), powdered
1 tsp red chilli powder
Salt to taste

- Wash spinach and fenugreek leaves separately changing water 2-3 times till all the grit is washed away.

- Chop fenugreek leaves, rub in ¼ teaspoon salt firmly and then squeeze out the bitter juice.

- Chop spinach leaves and place in a pan. Cover pan and place on heat for 5-7 minutes.

- Add fenugreek leaves, mix together and cook covered, on low heat for 5 minutes, stirring occasionally.

- Heat oil in a pressure cooker, add ground paste and sauté for 2 minutes.

- Add chicken and continue to sauté for 3 minutes further.

- Mix in spinach and fenugreek and sauté for 2-3 minutes.

- Pour in ½ cup hot water and cook under pressure for 7-8 minutes.

- Remove from heat and cool. Check if chicken is tender.

- Cook uncovered for 1-2 minutes, stirring periodically. Taste to correct seasoning.

- Serve with rice or chapatti.

Variation: **Palak Methi Taridar (Fenugreek with Spinach)**
Use an additional one kg spinach in place of chicken and add 250 gms chopped fresh coriander leaves with the fenugreek.

BOMBAY DUCK AND
AUBERGINE CURRY

Serves: 6

4 Bombay duck (sooka boomla)
3 tbsp oil
1 large onion, chopped
6 cloves garlic, finely crushed
3 long aubergines (baingan), cut into 3-cm cubes
Salt to taste, if required
2 tbsp freshly grated coconut

Mixed together to a paste:
½ tsp coriander powder
½ tsp turmeric powder
½ tsp cumin powder
½ tsp red chilli powder
2 tbsp malt vinegar

- Remove heads and fins of Bombay duck. Soak in water for 30 minutes. Drain, cut into quarters and brown lightly with a little oil in a pan, over low heat.

- Heat oil in a pan and sauté onion till golden. Add garlic and fry for ½ minute. Mix in masala paste and fry for 2-3 minutes.

- Add aubergines and sauté gently for 2 minutes. Stir in one cup water and cook till tender.

- Add fish and stir gently. Cover pan and simmer for 2 minutes. Add salt if needed.

- Reheat curry, mix in grated coconut and serve hot with rice, vegetables and any other curry.

KARELA-KA-CHILKA BHUNA

Crisp-fried Skin of Bitter Gourd

Makes: 1 cup

1 cup seeds and scraped skin of bitter gourds (karela)
½ tsp salt
1 tbsp mustard oil
2 dry red chillies, broken into pieces
2 onions, coarsely chopped
½ tsp turmeric powder

- Chop skin of bitter gourd, mix with seeds and salt and set aside.
- Heat oil till it smokes. Remove from heat and add chillies.
- Return to heat, add onions and fry till golden.
- Sprinkle in turmeric and fry for one minute.
- Add skin and seeds of bitter gourd and stir-fry for 5-7 minutes, making them crisp.
- Remove from heat.
- Serve with rice and a dal.

PAKODIVALI KADHI
Curd Sauce with Gram Flour Dumplings
Serves: 6

Kadhi:

½ cup gram flour (besan)
1 tsp turmeric powder
1 tsp salt
2 cups sour curd, beaten till smooth

Tempering:

2 tbsp oil
A pinch of powdered asafoetida (hing)
½ tsp cumin seeds
¼ tsp fenugreek seeds (methi)
4 dry red chillies

Pakodi:

1 cup gram flour (besan)
1½ tsp salt
½ tsp baking powder
½ cup oil

- Mix gram flour, turmeric powder and salt for kadhi.

- Add one cup curd and mix to a smooth paste.

- Add remaining curd and mix well. Stir in one litre water to make a thin mixture, ensuring that no lumps are formed.

- Heat oil for tempering in a large pan and add asafoetida, cumin seeds, fenugreek and red chillies. Stir-fry for ½ minute.

- Add curd mixture and stir constantly over medium heat for about 15 minutes, till mixture thickens. Remove from heat and set aside.

- Mix together gram flour, salt and baking powder for pakodi. Add enough water to make a thick batter. Whisk batter to a smooth consistency, cover and rest for one hour.

- Heat oil in a kadhai or deep frying pan till it smokes.

- Mix batter again. Drop spoonfuls of batter into oil and fry in batches, till golden. Drain and set aside.

- Add fried pakodi to kadhi and cook for 10 minutes just before serving.

- Serve with boiled rice.

KATHAL CURRY

Curried Green Jackfruit

Serves: 6

1 kg green jackfruit (kathal)
4 tbsp oil
4 medium-sized potatoes, peeled and cut into 3-cm cubes
½ tsp sugar
Salt to taste
1 tsp garam masala powder

Ground together with a little water:
3 dry red chillies
1 tbsp cumin seeds
1 tbsp coriander seeds
½ tsp turmeric powder

Tempering:
1 tbsp ghee
2-3 bay leaves (tej patta)
¼ tsp cumin seeds

- Peel the outer skin of jackfruit. Remove seeds, if any. Discard the fibrous portion, retaining only the 'meaty' portion. There is a layer of skin between the seed and the fruit. Ensure that this is also removed and discarded.

- Cut jackfruit into bite-sized pieces. Place in a pan with water and boil for about 15 minutes. Remove from heat. Drain well.

- Heat oil in a kadhai or deep frying pan. Fry potatoes until lightly browned. Remove from pan, drain and set aside.

- Add jackfruit and sauté for a few minutes. Remove from pan, drain and set aside.

- Add ground paste, sugar and salt to pan. Stir well and fry for several minutes, sprinkling water when necessary.

- Stir in 1½ cups water and add jackfruit and potatoes. Simmer gently until both are cooked and there is gravy in the pan.

- Heat ghee for tempering in a separate pan or kadhai. Add bay leaves and cumin. Stir-fry until they stop spluttering. Pour on to the vegetables and sprinkle in garam masala powder. Stir well and cook for a minute longer.

- Serve hot with rice or chapatti.

Sweets & Desserts

The most delicious and the healthiest desserts at any time of the year are made from fruits. In India, we get delicious fruits in summer, the most wonderful of all being the mango in all its varieties. There are nearly a thousand varieties of mangoes in the world and the largest range is grown in India.

Last year Sonal Mansingh, the well-known Odissi dancer, arrived from her mother's place in Saputara, laden with mangoes. Her dining room became the ripening chamber. Mangoes were spread out on mats, discreetly covered with bed covers. For a few friends—and I was luckily one of them—Sonal offered a mango feast and selected a variety for us to take back home.

I remember how Kamaladevi Chattopadhyay loved mangoes so much that during the season, if anyone invited her for a meal, she would say, 'Don't bother to cook, just give me mangoes to eat!'

I have always loved the small mangoes—sweet and juicy, ideal for sucking—which are not greatly valued by the connoisseurs. The delicious rasabara of Hyderabad really needs to be eaten in privacy since you require to be wrapped in a towel as you attack the mango. It is fibrous, juicy, thin-skinned and cannot be cut. By the time you finish eating it, which you will, for once you taste it you cannot put it down, you will need a bath. Then there is the langda with an unusual tang and aftertaste, which all langda fans adore, and the dusseheri, specially the tapka dusseheri, which was ripened on the tree and allowed to fall on mattresses kept below. An admirer from Meerut in the good old days used to send me a basket of the tapka dusseheri, which I used to eat secretly, like a miser. The alphonso, also known as hapus, is one of the most important commercial varieties of mango. It is fragrant, juicy and fleshy. Andhra Pradesh has the richest and most delicious mangoes—the begampali, the shah pasand and innumerable others. Last of all, to end the season, comes the chaunsa, golden-yellow, delicious and sweet.

There is also a range of melons: hindawana, green outside and a brilliant red inside; sarda, yellow, juicy and fragrant; the Lucknowi kharbooza; and the honey melon. These days we have a greater variety than before. Babar would not have complained that 'even India's melons are not sweet', if he had tasted the green striped watermelons.

There are also the litchis, falsa and jamun. From the mountains come the peaches and the strawberries. I prepare a number of desserts from these fruits as they are in season and therefore the best to eat. They are also cooling and ideal to have after a meal.

Round luscious peaches can be eaten just as they are. Recently peaches grown in the plains have become available in markets around the country. In Delhi, the well-to-do grow beautiful flowering peach trees in their farmhouses. The fruits are small and slightly bitter. There is also another larger variety, which is not really sweet, but tastes fresh and makes a good dessert.

WATERMELON CUP

Serves: 6

3 kg watermelon, oval-shaped, if possible
3 tbsp sugar syrup made with 2 tbsp water and 2 tbsp sugar, if
required
3 tbsp black currants washed and soaked in water for 1 hour
3 tsp Contreau

- With a sharp, long knife make an oval opening in the watermelon, leaving three-quarters of the melon intact, and remove the top.

- With a circular spoon, take out round spheres of the flesh. If it is too difficult to do so, cut melon into bite-sized pieces.

- Remove seeds and taste for sweetness; if not naturally sweet, add sugar syrup.

- Mix in black currants and Contreau gently. Place in the refrigerator in a bowl.

- Cut an oval hole in the middle of the smaller section of the melon rind to make a stand and place the larger melon section, which will serve as a bowl, over it.

- Pour in chilled melon into the melon bowl and serve directly on the table.

MIXED MELON CUP

Serves: 6

1 watermelon (about 2 kg)
1 marsh melon (about 1 kg)
3 tbsp sugar syrup made with 2 tbsp sugar and 2 tbsp water
Powdered seeds of 6 green cardamoms
¼ tsp angostura bitters
6 almonds, soaked in water, peeled and slivered

· Cut watermelon as given in watermelon cup (p. 164). Remove the red flesh, cut into bite-sized pieces and remove seeds.

· Cut marsh melon flesh into bite-sized pieces and mix with watermelon.

· Mix sugar syrup, cardamom powder and angostura bitters together and pour over melon. Sprinkle in two-thirds of the almonds and mix.

· Chill in the refrigerator.

· Prepare watermelon stand and bowl as given in watermelon cup and pour chilled melon into it. Sprinkle remaining almonds on top and serve immediately.

SWEET RICE AND MANGO

Serves: 6

2 kg sweet, firm mangoes
1 kg small, juicy mangoes
2 cups boiled, long-grained rice
4 tbsp powdered palm sugar (tardh gurd)
2 tbsp peanuts, freshly roasted, peeled and crushed

· Peel and cut the firm mangoes into bite-sized pieces and refrigerate. Peel the juicy mangoes, extract pulp, purée in a food processor and strain to remove fibres.

· Mix mango juice with rice and arrange in a ring on a flat, round, white dish.

· Dissolve sugar with ¼ cup water over low heat. Add peanuts, cook for 2 minutes and pour over rice.

· Fill the central portion of rice ring and encircle it with mango pieces and serve immediately.

MANGO CUP

Serves: 6

2 kg ripe, sweet mangoes
½ litre (2¼ cups) milk
2 tbsp pistachio kernels, cut into thin slivers

· Peel mangoes, cut and blend with milk in a food processor.

· Pour into coupe cups or glass bowls, sprinkle with pistachios and chill before serving.

LITCHIS WITH
ICE CREAM

Serves: 6

1 kg litchis
4 tbsp sugar
½ tsp vanilla
1 litre vanilla ice cream
6 tsp brandy

· Peel and deseed litchis.

· Dissolve sugar in one cup water over heat and cook for 10 minutes to make a light syrup. Add vanilla and litchis.

· Cook for 5 minutes on medium heat, allow to cool and chill.

· Serve 3 scoops of ice cream into large individual bowls, add litchis, sprinkle over one teaspoon brandy and enjoy.

GOLDEN PEACH DESSERT

Serves: 6

I recently tasted a delicious dessert of lightly stewed peaches filled with a crunchy array of some delicacy. Since the lady was very cagey about giving the recipe, I improvised:

3 large peaches
4 tbsp sugar
4 green cardamoms
4 cloves
3-cm stick cinnamon
2 tbsp jaggery, crushed
6 almonds, coarsely crushed
3 walnuts, coarsely crushed
6 tsp brandy

- Place peaches in boiling water for a few minutes. Drain and plunge into ice-cold water. Remove from water when cool and peel. Cut in half, carefully separate halves and discard seed.

- Add one cup water, sugar and spices to a pan on heat, stir till sugar has dissolved, and boil for 7-8 minutes.

- Lower peaches into syrup and cook for 5-6 minutes on low heat, until cooked but firm. Remove pan from heat and set aside.

- Melt jaggery in a pan over heat, add almonds and walnuts and stir together until well mixed.

- Place peaches in a glass bowl, strain syrup around peaches and scoop nuts into the peach hollows. Add one teaspoon brandy to each and serve at room temperature.

Monsoon

After the burning, searing heat of the summer, the rains come with a great deal of drama—darkening clouds, thunder, lightning flashes and peacocks madly calling out 'peo peo'. The birds twitter and the pipal leaves curl upwards to catch the first drops of rain. In my youth, we would all run out to feel the first rain on our parched bodies. In the rural areas, people greet the first rains with joy and dance gaily in the rain to pulsating drum beats.

One of the folk songs sung during this time carries the rhythm of gathering dark clouds, the flailing wind and the falling rain in which the young women's colourful veils fly:

Ghan Ghor Ghurva
Jhak Jhor Purva
Aou banki chunar lahriya
Pheraya rasai

Ashadh is the beginning of the monsoon season. It is the month before Sawan, which is the main month of the rains. It is the time of special festivals, like teej, the festival of women. The men put up swings and the women go out in groups singing, dressed in their best, and swinging high up into the branches of the trees, carefree, full of laughter and joy, away from the narrow confines of their marital home, where they have to conform to formal behaviour in front of the elders.

Monsoon is the season of ecstasy and prohibitions. Luckily, nowadays the prohibitions are only for those who have already given up the world. The Jain sadhu and sadhavi live an ascetic life where most of the time is spent in fasting and observing various prohibitions, like travelling. The food restrictions are also many.

This was the season when people would make special savouries—pakodé or fried fritters—to celebrate the rains and gurd purdha or pancakes, with a sprinkling of aniseed for flavouring and to help with the digestion. However, these are also the days when we have to be careful with our food. Leftovers are best avoided and a number of food items are omitted from the diet.

I generally don't serve cold soups and uncooked salads during the monsoon. I serve a main dish with possibly chicken, some mince or meat, a few dal preparations and a number of vegetables. Those who like soups and salads should have them hot and use cooked vegetables.

According to the Ayurvedic system, leafy green vegetables are to be avoided, as also vegetables that cause flatulence, such as potatoes, cabbage and colocasia. It is also believed that mandagini—the body heat—is at a low ebb and thus heating items like ginger, garlic, chillies, black pepper and whole spices should be used. During the day, fried dishes are supposed to be good and, strangely enough, we are advised to pour a little ghee on the food. Curd is also considered good, but can be eaten only during the day. Chahivala gosht—meat cooked in buttermilk—is ideal for this weather. Though sweets may be taken, those made from thickened milk are not recommended, as digesting them would be difficult. These are the months when fish is avoided, though you can eat dried fish.

Soups, Salads & Starters

EGG SOUP WITH TOMATO

Serves: 6

This is a soup that can be made in an instant. If boiled noodles and rice are added to it, and served along with a cooked salad, it makes a refreshing and substantial meal.

1 tbsp butter
1 small onion, finely chopped
6 cloves garlic, finely crushed
6 cups water
3 chicken *or* vegetable soup cubes
3-4 lemon grass stalks, tied together
1 tsp salt
½ tsp brown sugar
½ tsp light soya sauce
1 tbsp sherry *or* 2 tbsp red wine
3 eggs, lightly beaten
3 large tomatoes, blanched, peeled and cut into wedges
½ cup chopped spring onions (optional)
¼ cup chopped fresh coriander leaves

- Melt butter in a large pan and sauté onion till golden. Add garlic and sauté for ½ minute. Add remaining ingredients except eggs, tomatoes, spring onions and coriander leaves.

- Slowly pour eggs into hot soup. Allow to set and stir after one minute.

- Add tomatoes and cook for 3 minutes.

- Mix in spring onions and cook for 2 minutes. Add coriander and stir for a minute.

- Taste for flavour, adjust seasoning and serve hot.

BOTTLE GOURD SALAD

Serves: 6

Bottle gourd, known as ghia or lauki, is a summer and monsoon vegetable and is prescribed by naturopaths and vaids—Ayurvedic practitioners—as an important part of our diet. It is easy to digest and has calcium, phosphorus, potassium, sulphur and vitamin C. It has curative values for a number of stomach and kidney problems. It is a vegetable that needs to be cooked with other vegetables to give it flavour, as it is quite bland.

1 kg bottle gourd (lauki), preferably the round variety
Oil for coating gourd
1 onion, chopped
2-cm piece fresh ginger, finely grated and soaked in 1 tbsp lime juice
¼ cup chopped fresh mint leaves
Salt and pepper to taste
2 tbsp lime juice

- Rub oil over bottle gourd and roast over a live flame until skin is burnt.

- Peel and cut into small pieces. Remove and discard pockets of seeds, if any, and mash flesh.

- Add onion, ginger, mint, salt and pepper to bottle gourd and mix with lime juice.

- Place in a salad bowl and serve cold or at room temperature.

PUMPKIN SALAD

Serves: 4

This is a very refreshing salad and can be served during all seasons. However, monsoon is the best time as it is easy to digest. It is also ideal to serve at the spring festival of Vasant Panchami.

¾ kg yellow pumpkin (kaddu)
¾ tsp salt *or* to taste
1½ tbsp very finely chopped onion
1½ tbsp finely chopped fresh coriander leaves
1½ tbsp finely chopped green chillies
4-6 tbsp curd, beaten till smooth

- Remove seeds and skin from pumpkin and cut into small pieces.
- Place in a pan with ¼ cup water and salt. Cook covered, till pumpkin is very soft. Uncover pan and continue cooking till it is dry.
- Mash pumpkin to a smooth pulp with a potato masher or fork. Allow to cool and add remaining ingredients.
- Mix well and put into a serving dish.
- Refrigerate for one hour before serving.

Cooking for All Seasons

MUSHROOM PÂTÉ

Serves: 6

½ kg mushrooms
3 tbsp butter
6 cloves garlic, finely chopped
¾ tsp salt
½ tsp pepper
¼ tsp powdered allspice (kabab cheeni)
2 tbsp malt vinegar
2 tbsp red wine
Extra butter for covering pâté

· Soak mushrooms in warm water for 10 minutes and wash thoroughly under running water. Drain, chop and set aside.

· Melt butter in a pan, add garlic and sauté till golden. Add mushroom and sauté for 5 minutes.

· Stir in salt, pepper, allspice and vinegar and cook covered for 5 minutes.

· Cool and grind to a paste with wine.

· Check for flavour. It should be delicately seasoned.

· Pour into a mould, cover with melted butter and store in a refrigerator overnight.

· Unmould and serve with crisp bread.

Meat, Chicken, Fish & Vegetables

GOLDEN MOUSSAKA
Baked Bottle Gourd, Pumpkin and Mince

Serves: 6

1 kg bottle gourd (lauki)
1 kg yellow pumpkin (kaddu)
Salt as required
Oil for shallow-frying
¼ cup butter
2 large onions, finely chopped
750 gms mince
½ cup white wine
1½ tsp salt
1 tsp pepper
¼ tsp powdered nutmeg
2 tomatoes, chopped
3 medium-sized onions, cut into rings and fried crisp
3 cups béchamel sauce (p. 234)
¼ cup grated cheddar cheese
¼ cup chopped fresh mint leaves
Extra butter for greasing dish and dotting over moussaka

- Peel and cut bottle gourd and pumpkin into slices, sprinkle with salt and set aside for one hour. Drain and dry in a towel.

- Heat oil for shallow-frying in a frying pan, and fry bottle gourd and pumpkin for 5 minutes. Drain and set aside.

- Heat butter in another pan and sauté chopped onions for 2 minutes.

- Add mince and cook for 10-15 minutes.

- Add wine, salt, pepper, nutmeg and tomatoes and simmer for 30 minutes. Remove from heat.

- Take a well-buttered baking dish and arrange half the vegetables in the dish. Sprinkle with fried onion rings.

- Cover with mince, place remaining vegetables on top and cover with béchamel sauce.

- Sprinkle cheese and mint on top, and dot with small nuts of butter.

- Bake in a moderate oven at 200°C (400°F) for 30 minutes. Serve hot.

HOT-POT OF BEAN CURD
AND VEGETABLES

Serves: 6

This hot-pot has a delicious fresh taste. It is best cooked in a clay or earthenware pot, but you can also use a casserole.

8 cups chicken stock *or* 4 chicken cubes dissolved in 8 cups water
10 dried mushrooms soaked in hot water for 2 hours, drained and chopped
1 carrot, scraped and sliced into thin rounds
4 spring onions, chopped
½ cup canned bamboo shoots, thinly sliced
2 tbsp cloud-ear fungus, soaked for ½ hour, drained and sliced into thin strips
300 gms bean curd, cut into 2-cm squares
250 gms chicken liver, cleaned and sliced
1 tsp light soya sauce
1 tsp malt vinegar
1 tsp salt

- Bring stock to boil in a clay or earthenware pot and put in mushrooms, carrot, spring onions, bamboo shoot and fungus. Bring to boil and continue boiling for 10 minutes.

- Add bean curd and chicken liver. Simmer for another 10 minutes. Season with soya sauce, vinegar and salt.

- Serve hot with steamed rice.

Note: For those who prefer a hot dish add chilli sauce and more soya sauce.

Cloud-ear fungus is available in shops specializing in oriental foodstuff.

RICE-NOODLES AND NONYA SAUCE WITH COCONUT

Serves: 4

Laksa or rice-noodles eaten with a chicken and vegetable sauce and sprouted beans is a meal in itself. Fine rice vermicelli is now available in shops in India.

My favourite sauce is nonya sauce with coconut.

250 gms fine rice vermicelli *or* any other noodles
1 cup bean sprouts

Nonya sauce:

1 spring chicken (about 500 gms), cut into small pieces
Salt as required
2 tbsp oil
2 cups coconut milk, made from 2 fresh coconuts
2 cucumbers, peeled, seeded and cut into juliennes
250 gms spring onions, finely chopped

Ground to a paste:

1 onion
5-cm piece fresh ginger
5 cloves garlic
3 dry red chillies
4 dry shrimps, roasted and chopped
1 tsp turmeric powder
1 tsp coriander powder

· Place chicken with 4 cups water and one teaspoon salt in a pan. Cook for 15 minutes till tender. Drain and reserve stock. Remove meat from bones and discard bones.

- Heat oil in a pan and fry ground paste for 2 minutes. Add chicken and fry lightly for 4-5 minutes.

- Stir in coconut milk and reserved stock. Add cucumbers and cook on low heat for 5 minutes.

- Add spring onions and cook for one minute further. Taste and adjust seasoning.

- Semi-cook vermicelli and just before serving, place it in a large pan. Pour over boiling water to cover vermicelli completely. Cover pan and leave for 8-10 minutes. Drain and place in individual bowls.

- If using egg noodles or thick rice-noodles, boil in salted water till done, drain and place in individual bowls.

- Pour boiling water over bean sprouts and leave for 2-3 minutes. Drain and place on top of noodles.

- Pour sauce over noodles and bean sprouts and serve with chilli and soya sauce on the side.

Variation: Add tamarind to make the sauce hot, sweet and sour. You can also vary the vegetables by adding boiled zucchini, celery and bean curd as well as French beans.

KWAY SWE

Burmese Chicken Curry with Noodles

Serves: 6

The first time I tasted this wonderful dish was at the home of the great sculptor S.L. Prashar. His wife's family had lived in Burma and this dish was made especially for our delectation. Prashar Sahib, as we called him, was a vegetarian, but he took great pleasure in seeing others enjoy their meal.

In Kway Swe the main dish is the curry and it is served with hot boiled noodles and a range of accompaniments.

1 chicken (about 1¼ kg), skinned and cut into pieces
1 tsp salt
1 tsp pepper
1 tsp turmeric powder
1 tsp coriander powder
1 tsp cumin powder
5 tbsp oil
3 tbsp lime juice
2 cups coconut cream *or* coconut milk made from 2 coconuts
2 kg noodles

Ground to a paste:
2 medium-sized onions
10 cloves garlic
4-cm piece fresh ginger
3 green chillies
10 dried prawns, roasted

Accompaniments for serving with curry:
1 cup chopped spring onions
½ cup chopped fresh coriander leaves
4 eggs, hard-boiled and chopped
½ cup finely sliced onions, fried crisp

¼ cup finely chopped garlic, fried till golden
15 dry prawns, roasted, crushed and ground with 6 roasted dry red
chillies, salt to taste and ½ cup vinegar
8 tbsp soya sauce
½ cup chilli sauce

- Rub chicken with salt and pepper, place in a pan and cover with water. Add turmeric, coriander and cumin and cook till chicken is tender.

- Drain. Remove meat from bones, reserve stock and discard bones.

- Add 3 tablespoons oil to a pan and fry ground paste for 5 minutes.

- Add chicken and sauté for 5 minutes, adding stock as required, so that it does not burn. Stir in remaining stock and lime juice and simmer for a few minutes.

- Add coconut cream. Lower heat and simmer for 5 minutes further. Check seasoning and adjust.

- Fill ¾ of a large pan with water and bring to boil.

- Add one tablespoon salt, 2 tablespoons oil and ⅓ of the noodles. Cook till soft, but not soggy. Drain over another large pan and place it on heat, adding additional water for the next batch.

- Serve hot noodles and half the hot chicken curry with the different accompaniments arranged on the table.

- Replenish noodles and chicken curry as required.

- Noodles are placed in individual bowls, covered with chicken curry and sprinkled with accompaniments, according to taste.

BHINDI AUR MURGH
Chicken with Okra

Serves: 4

1 large chicken (about 1¼ kg), without skin
Oil *or* ghee as needed
2 medium-sized onions, finely sliced
2-3 whole dry red chillies
5-cm stick cinnamon
Salt as required
¾ kg okra (bhindi), cut into 2-cm pieces

Ground to a paste:

6-8 cloves garlic
3-cm piece fresh ginger

- Cut chicken into small pieces and set aside.
- Heat 2 tablespoons oil in a pan and fry onions till deep golden. Add ground paste and cook for one minute.
- Add chicken and sauté till lightly browned.
- Add chillies, cinnamon, 1½ cups water and 1¼ teaspoons salt.
- Bring to boil, lower heat and simmer covered, till chicken is tender and about one cup gravy remains.
- Pour oil or ghee to a depth of one-cm into a frying pan and heat. Add okra and fry till crisp. Remove from pan, drain and sprinkle salt.
- Mix okra with chicken and cook on medium heat for 10 minutes.
- Serve with rice and any raita of your choice.

CHICKEN WITH SESAME AND MUSTARD SAUCE

Serves: 6

1 kg chicken breast
1 onion, thickly sliced
6 cloves garlic, thickly sliced
4 lemon grass stalks, tied in a bundle
Salt as required
4 tbsp sesame seeds (til), dry roasted
4 tsp chilli-hot oriental sesame oil
1 tbsp sweet soya sauce
3 tbsp hot mustard powder
5 tbsp corn oil
3 tsp chilli-hot oil
100 gms fun sie (cellophane noodles)
3 spring onions, chopped

- Place chicken, onion, garlic, lemon grass, ½ teaspoon salt and 2 cups water in a pan. Bring to boil, lower heat and simmer for about 15 minutes, till chicken is tender.

- Drain chicken. Discard onion, garlic and lemon grass and reserve stock for sauce and other purposes.

- Slice chicken into thin strips and keep warm.

- Reserve one teaspoon sesame seeds and crush remaining to a fine paste. Mix with sesame oil, sweet soya sauce and one teaspoon salt. Stir in just enough stock to make a pouring sauce.

- Mix mustard with corn oil, chilli-hot oil and ½ tsp salt and blend together. If necessary, add stock to make a pouring sauce.

- Soak noodles in boiling water for 10 minutes until softened. Drain and place in a dish.
- Mix chicken with spring onions and lay it over the noodles. Pour over half of both sauces, sprinkle with remaining sesame seeds and serve with remaining sauces placed in individual jugs for additional serving.

CAPTAIN'S CURRY

Serves: 6

1 chicken (about 1 kg)
3 tbsp oil
1 tsp turmeric powder
1 tsp salt
2 tsp jaggery, crushed
1½ cups coconut milk made from 1½ fresh coconuts

Dry roasted and ground to a paste with 2 tbsp lime juice for marinade:

6 dried shrimps
10-cm lemon grass stalk, finely chopped
1 tbsp whole coriander seeds
1 tsp cumin seeds
¼ tsp fenugreek seeds (methi)
6 dry red chillies

Ground together to a paste:

2 large onions
6 cloves garlic
5-cm piece fresh ginger

- Cut chicken into 5-cm pieces, rub in marinade and allow to marinate for about 2 hours.

- Sauté onion paste in oil for 2-3 minutes. Add turmeric powder and stir-fry for one minute. Add chicken and continue to stir-fry for 5-6 minutes. Add salt and jaggery, and stir in coconut milk. Simmer on low heat till chicken is tender and sauce has thickened.

- Serve with rice and a bitter gourd preparation, to help digestion.

DRIED FISH AND TOMATO CURRY

Serves: 4

250 gms dried salted fish (not Bombay duck *or* shrimps)
3 tbsp oil
1 large onion, sliced
6 cloves garlic, crushed
1 kg (12 large) tomatoes, chopped
2 tsp malt vinegar
4 green chillies, slit lengthwise
½ tsp coconut powder
Salt for seasoning, if necessary
2 tbsp chopped fresh coriander leaves

Mixed to a paste with a little water:
1 tsp turmeric powder
½ tsp cumin powder
½ tsp coriander powder
½ tsp red chilli powder

- Wash fish and, if large, cut into small pieces. Soak in water for one hour. Drain and wash again.

- Heat oil in a pan and fry masala paste for 1-2 minutes, till oil separates. Add onion and garlic and sauté till golden brown. Mix in tomatoes and sauté for 2 minutes.

- Add fish and fry for 2-3 minutes. Add vinegar and one cup water and simmer for 5 minutes. Stir in chillies and coconut and simmer on low heat for 5 minutes.

- Check salt and add if needed. Sprinkle in coriander leaves and serve.

KIHIM SUKHI JHINGA BHUJIA

Curried Dried Shrimps

Serves: 4

My friend Salima Tayabji's home in Kihim is a paradise on earth. Her mali's wife, Savitri, used to serve us fried dried shrimps with rice-flour chapatti for breakfast.

1 cup dry shrimps
2 tbsp oil
2 onions, finely chopped .
8 cloves garlic, finely chopped
¼ tsp turmeric powder
½ tsp coriander powder
½ tsp cumin powder
½ tsp red chilli powder
4 green chillies, chopped
3 tomatoes, finely chopped

· Wash shrimps in plenty of water, rubbing them between your hands. Drain and repeat with fresh water. Soak in water for 30 minutes.

· Heat oil in a kadhai or deep frying pan and fry onions and garlic till golden. Sprinkle in spice powders and sauté briskly for ½ minute. Drain shrimps and add. Sauté for 5 minutes.

· Stir in chillies and tomatoes. Cover pan and cook on low heat for 5 minutes. Check that it does not catch at the base. Open pan and cook till liquid has dried.

· Serve with naan or chapatti.

SURJAN KE PATTÉ KI SABZI

Fried Drumstick Leaves

Serves: 4

Drumstick leaves eaten before the beginning of a meal with rice or chapatti is an excellent antidote to blood pressure, diabetes and indigestion.

In many parts of India the drumstick tree is an essential part of the kitchen garden. The leaves, flowers and the drumsticks can be eaten and are excellent for health.

2 cups leaves of drumstick tree
2 tbsp mustard oil
2 dry red chillies, broken into pieces
1 tsp panch poran (Bengal 5-spice mixture)
1 large onion, sliced
½ tsp salt

- Wash leaves to take out all grit, drain well and set aside.

- Heat oil in a pan till it smokes. Remove from heat. Add chillies and panch poran.

- Return pan to heat and stir till spices splutter.

- Add onion and stir-fry for 2 minutes.

- Mix in drumstick leaves and stir-fry for a further 5 minutes.

- Serve with rice or chapatti along with any other dishes.

D O H R O O

Sweet and Sour Drumsticks – Parsi Style

Serves: 4

50 gms tamarind (the size of a golf ball), soaked in 1 cup hot water
for 15 minutes
¼ kg jaggery, grated or cut very fine
4 drumsticks, peeled and cut into 7-cm pieces
1 tsp salt *or* to taste
2 tbsp oil *or* ghee
1 medium-sized onion, finely sliced
1 tsp cumin seeds
½ tsp cumin powder
½ tsp turmeric powder
1 tsp garam masala powder
1 tsp ground black pepper
1-cm piece fresh ginger, finely chopped
2-3 green chillies, finely chopped
1 tbsp chopped fresh coriander leaves
1½ tbsp gram flour (besan)
1 medium-sized tomato, blanched, peeled and cut into 6 pieces each

- Extract tamarind juice, add jaggery and set aside for 30 minutes.

- Tie drumsticks into bundles of 3-4 pieces and boil in water with ½ tsp salt, till they are cooked. Drain and set aside.

- Heat oil or ghee in a pan and fry onion till brown.

- Add cumin seeds, powdered spices, ginger, green chillies and coriander leaves and cook for one minute.

- Sprinkle in gram flour, pour in ¾ cup water and cook for one minute, stirring continuously.

- Add tomato and mix. Stir in tamarind juice and jaggery with ½ tsp salt.

- Add drumsticks, bring to boil, lower heat and simmer covered for 5 minutes.

- Serve hot with rice, papad and a salad.

HAAQ SAAG

Savoury Kashmir Greens

Serves: 6

2 kg haaq greens
3 tbsp mustard oil
¼ tsp powdered asafoetida (hing)
4 dry red chillies
1 tsp dry ginger powder (saunth)
1 tsp aniseed (saunf), powdered
½ tsp red chilli powder
1½ tsp salt

- Wash greens to remove all grit. Discard thick stems and coarsely chop tender stems and leaves.

- Heat oil in a pressure cooker till it smokes. Lower heat and add asafoetida and red chillies. Stir for ¼ minute.

- Add remaining ingredients with ½ cup hot water.

- Close cooker and cook under pressure for 10 minutes.

- Cool and open cooker.

- Serve hot with boiled rice along with any other dishes.

Note: The Kashmiri Pandits though not always vegetarians do not eat garlic and onions.

KARELA BHARWÉ
Bitter Gourds Stuffed with Potatoes
Serves: 4

8 (about ½ kg) bitter gourds (karela)
1 tsp salt
2 tbsp oil

Marinade:

1½ cups curd, beaten till smooth
1 tsp red chilli powder
½ tsp turmeric powder

Stuffing:

2 tbsp oil
2 medium-sized onions, grated
6 cloves garlic, ground
2-cm piece fresh ginger, ground
2 medium-sized potatoes, boiled and mashed
Tamarind pulp made with a lime-sized ball of tamarind and 2 tbsp
water
½ tsp salt

· Scrape bitter gourds, removing rough outer skin. Slit
  lengthwise and remove seeds. Reserve the skin and
  seeds for karela-ka-chilka bhuna (p. 157).

· Place bitter gourds into a pan with salt, cover with
  cold water and bring to boil. Boil for 1-2 minutes,
  drain and squeeze out thoroughly to remove the
  bitter juice.

· Mix ingredients for marinade, rub over bitter gourds
  and allow to marinate for one hour.

- Heat oil for stuffing in a pan and fry onions till pale gold.
- Add garlic and ginger and sauté for one minute.
- Remove pan from heat and mix in mashed potatoes, tamarind pulp and salt.
- Stuff bitter gourds with this mixture and tie with white cotton thread to prevent stuffing from coming out.
- Heat 2 tablespoons oil in a frying pan. Place bitter gourds in a single layer in the pan and fry on all sides till brown.
- Pour any remaining marinade over bitter gourds. Cover pan and cook over moderate heat, turning bitter gourds once, till liquid dries.
- Serve hot with chapatti or rice along with any other dishes.

MAJI'S FRIED CURD

Serves: 6

This is an easy, quick dish to make and can even replace the andé ki bhujia—spiced scrambled eggs—the easy standby for unexpected guests, in a north Indian home.

This was made by my mother in Abbotabad where vegetables were scarce.

3 cups curd, at room temperature
½ tsp red chilli powder
1½ tsp salt *or* to taste
1 tbsp butter
1 large onion, finely chopped
3-cm piece fresh ginger, finely chopped
¾ tsp turmeric powder
3 green chillies, finely chopped (optional)
1½ tsp cumin seeds
3 tbsp finely chopped fresh coriander leaves

- Beat curd with chilli powder and salt till smooth and well blended, and set aside.

- Melt butter in a pan and fry onion and ginger till golden. Add remaining ingredients except curd. Stir and cook until the aroma of turmeric comes up.

- Remove from heat and slowly add curd, stirring all the while. Serve immediately.

Note: If you wish to heat the curd mixture, warm it gently. Do not allow it to boil, otherwise it will curdle.

BEAN CURD WITH DRIED MUSHROOMS

Serves: 6

500 gms bean curd
½ cup oil for deep-frying
8 dried mushrooms, soaked for 2 hours
200 gms spring onions with greens
3 green chillies, finely chopped
1 tbsp soya sauce
1 tbsp oyster sauce
1 tsp sugar
1 tsp salt
1 cup chicken stock *or* water
2 tsp cornflour
1 tsp chilli-hot oriental sesame oil

- Cut bean curd into 3-cm squares and set aside.

- Place oil for deep-frying in a kadhai or wok and heat to smoking point.

- Lower heat, place bean curd in a slotted spoon and lower into oil. Fry in batches till dark brown. Remove from oil and drain.

- Drain mushroom, cut stems and slice into fine, long pieces.

- Cut the white section of spring onions into round slices about one cm thick and the green stalks 4 cm long.

- In another pan, heat 2 tablespoons of the oil used to fry bean curd, add mushrooms, spring onions and green chillies and sauté for 3 minutes.

- Add the sauces, sugar, salt and stock or water. Cook covered until mushrooms are tender.

- Add bean curd and cook covered for 3 minutes further.

- Mix cornflour with ¼ cup water and stir into sauce. Continue stirring till sauce thickens.

- Sprinkle in chilli-hot sesame oil and serve.

FRIED BEAN CURD

Serves: 4

400 gms fresh bean curd
2 tbsp oil
1 onion, finely chopped
2 green chillies, finely chopped
2 tbsp fresh coriander leaves
½ tbsp sweet soya sauce
1 tbsp regular soya sauce
1 tbsp malt vinegar
Salt to taste

- Cut bean curd into 5-cm squares.

- Heat oil in a pan and fry onion till golden.

- Add remaining ingredients except bean curd and salt and mix together.

- Add bean curd and sprinkle in salt. Mix gently by pouring sauce over bean curd with a spoon. Cover pan and simmer for 2 minutes.

- Serve hot with noodles or rice or as a side dish.

Sweets & Desserts

During the rainy season you have to eat lightly as it is difficult to digest rich food. Desserts also need to be light. I generally serve phirni or stewed apples, though the apples are often from the cold storage at this time of the year. Cream caramel is another favourite, as is lauki kheer and sweet raw papaya.

The first rains are celebrated by making purdha—wheat pancakes made with jaggery and aniseed.

BARASH KA PURDHA

Sweet Wheat Pancakes

Serves: 4

1 cup whole wheat flour (atta)
¼ cup powdered jaggery
1 tsp aniseed (saunf)
½ tsp baking powder
3 tbsp unsalted butter *or* 4 tbsp corn oil

- Mix one cup water slowly into the flour to make a smooth batter of pouring consistency. Add jaggery and mix well. Mix in aniseed and baking powder, cover with a napkin and set aside for one hour.

- Heat a non-stick frying pan and add one teaspoon butter. Melt butter, swivelling it around until the base of the pan is well coated.

- Stir batter well and when the butter is hot, pour in a ladle of batter. With the back of the ladle, make circular movements to spread it out thinly.

- Lower heat and cook till base is set. With a wooden spatula, check if the sides are done. Rotate pancake in the pan to ensure it does not stick to the pan. If necessary dribble in some more butter along the sides.

- Flip over, cook for 1-2 minutes further and remove from heat. Make remaining pancakes in the same way.

- Serve the purdha as they are being made. They should be eaten piping hot.

SEVIAN PAYASAM

Vermicelli Dessert

Serves: 6

175 gms vermicelli (use the packaged instant variety)
4 tsp ghee *or* melted unsalted butter
12 cashew nuts, halved
½ cup sugar
Powdered seeds of 6 green cardamoms
2 cups milk

- Heat ghee or butter in a frying pan and fry vermicelli to a reddish brown colour.
- Remove from frying pan and put into a wide pan.
- Fry cashew nuts in ghee or butter left over in the frying pan. Drain and set aside.
- Pour 2 cups boiling water over vermicelli and place pan on heat.
- Add remaining ingredients and cook for 5 minutes, or until sugar is dissolved.
- Serve at room temperature.

MOONG DAL PAYASAM

Green Bean Dessert

Serves: 6

1 cup split green beans (chilké ki moong dal)
1¼ cups powdered jaggery
2 cups milk
Powdered seeds of 8 green cardamoms
20 almonds, peeled and chopped

- Wash dal and place in a pan with 2 cups water. Place pan on heat and cook dal until it breaks up and is mixed to a smooth creamy consistency.

- Add jaggery and stir till dissolved.

- Add hot milk, stirring until it is well mixed together.

- Remove from heat, mix in cardamom powder and almonds and serve at room temperature.

Note: You may use whole green beans, in which case you will have to pressure-cook it for 10 minutes.

SEVIAN KA HALWA

Vermicelli Sweet

Serves: 4

175 gms vermicelli (use the packaged instant variety)
3 tbsp unsalted butter
1 cup sugar
¾ cup milk
1 tsp powdered green cardamom

Decoration:

2 tbsp almond slivers

- Melt butter in a pan and fry vermicelli to a golden brown colour. Remove from heat and set aside in the pan.

- Put sugar, milk and cardamom in another pan and cook, stirring till sugar has dissolved.

- Add to vermicelli and mix. Return pan with vermicelli to heat and stir with a lifting motion, so that vermicelli does not become lumpy.

- Cook till liquid had dried out.

- Place in a platter and serve with almonds sprinkled over the top.

MOONG DAL HALWA

Husked Green Bean Sweet

Serves: 4

1 cup husked green beans, (moong dal)
12 green cardamoms, seeds powdered and skins reserved
1½ cups sugar
½ cup melted butter
1 tsp gram flour (besan)
4 tbsp sultanas (kishmish), washed and soaked for 1 hour
⅓ cup almonds, peeled and sliced

· Soak dal overnight. The next day, drain dal, wash well and grind to a rough paste.

· Place cardamom skins into a pan with sugar and pour in 2 cups water. Place on heat and stir till sugar is dissolved. Continue to simmer for 2 minutes further. Remove from heat, discard cardamom skins and set aside the syrup.

· Heat butter in a kadhai or wok and fry gram flour till lightly browned.

· Remove from heat and add dal paste.

· Return to medium heat and cook, stirring constantly.

· Add sugar syrup slowly and continue to stir till the dal separates into granules.

· Add cardamom seeds and drained sultanas. Stir and cook till golden and the fat separates.

· Mix in almonds and cook for 1-2 minutes further.

GILL KI PHIRNI

Custard in Earthen Bowls

Serves: 6

Buy 6 small terracotta bowls or lids for pitchers from the local potter. See that they rest firmly on the base. Scrub with a scourer and soak overnight. In the morning, turn them upside down to drain water.

3 cups milk
6 tbsp sugar
3 tbsp arrowroot powder
4 tbsp rose water
4 green cardamoms, powdered

Decoration:

2 tbsp chopped pistachio

- Mix milk with sugar in a pan and place on heat. Stir till sugar is dissolved and add arrowroot powder and rose water.

- Lower heat and cook, stirring continuously—otherwise it will catch at the bottom—for 5-7 minutes.

- When the milk has thickened pour into the terracotta bowls and sprinkle pistachio on top.

- Place in a cool place to set.

- Serve each person in individual bowls.

- The smell of the wet earth gives an added allure to the phirni. Thus the name coined by me from gill ittar, the perfume of wet earth.

For All Seasons

Roti

CHAPATTI

Makes: 15-18 chapatti

The simplest and yet the most complicated thing to make is a simple round chapatti, which will puff up like a ball. Let me confess at the outset, I cannot make them perfectly round. I therefore generally make three cornered or square chapatti and parathé, or those that I can shape with my hands like tandoori roti and parathé, or makki ki roti.

2 cups whole wheat flour (atta)
½-¾ cup water
Extra flour for rolling chapatti

· Sift flour into a parat, thali or a flat round plate with a rim. Slowly add water and mix with your fingers, until the flour sticks together.

· Begin making it into a ball by rolling it on the surface of the plate.

· Knead for at least 6-7 minutes and place on one side of the plate. Cover with a damp cloth and set aside for at least one hour. It is now ready to be made into chapatti, roti or paratha, on the griddle as well as in the tandoor.

- Knead dough once again with damp hands. Sprinkle ½ cup flour on a flat tray, to use as you roll out the chapatti.

- Make small balls the size of a mandarin orange by rolling the dough into the palm of your hand. Place them in a separate plate. If not using immediately, cover with a damp cloth.

- Place one ball on the dry flour spread in the tray and press it down flattening it. Do the same with the other side. Now sprinkle dry flour on to a chakla or wooden board and roll it out using even pressure, to make a chapatti 12-15 cm in diameter. As you roll, dip the chapatti into the dry flour, as required, to prevent it from sticking.

- Place a tava or griddle, preferably one with a handle, on heat.

- Put a drop of water on the tava. When it sizzles, lower heat and place a chapatti on it. Cook for 2 minutes, pressing and rotating it with a folded tea towel. Turn over and cook the other side in the same manner. As you press and rotate, it will puff up.

STUFFED PARATHA

Makes: 8-10 parathé

Dough made with 2 cups whole wheat flour (atta) as given for
chapatti (p. 209)
Extra flour for rolling parathé
8-10 tsp oil for smearing parathé

Stuffing (any of the following):
2 potatoes, boiled and mashed
1 cup grated cauliflower
1 cup cooked dal of any kind
1 cup cooked mince

Mixed herbs and spices for stuffing:
1 green chilli, finely chopped
2 tbsp fresh coriander leaves, finely chopped
1 tsp dried pomegranate seeds (anardana), crushed
1 tbsp dry mango powder (amchur)
1 tsp salt

- Mix selected stuffing with mixed herbs and spices.

- Roll out 2 chapatti (p. 209).

- Sprinkle dry flour on a wooden board and place a chapatti on it. Spread one tablespoon of stuffing on chapatti, leaving ½ cm around the edge. Dip a finger in water and put a thin veneer of water around the edge. Place another chapatti on top, bring the edges of the second chapatti to meet the one below and press down to seal. Rotate the chapatti pressing down on it gently.

- Heat a tava or griddle. Put a drop of water on it and when it sizzles lower heat and put paratha on griddle.

Cook for 2 minutes, rotating it with a folded tea towel. Turn over and cook the other side. The first side should have brown spots on it.

- Spread ½ teaspoon oil over paratha and turn over. Spread another ½ teaspoon oil over the surface, rotating the paratha with the spoon. Lift off the griddle and put into a plate.

- Prepare remaining parathé in the same way.

KHAMEERI ROTI

Leavened Bread

Makes: 6 roti

1 cup whole wheat flour (atta)
½ tsp baking powder
½ tsp salt
¼ cup water

- Mix all ingredients together to make a dough. Knead well, wrap in a cloth and keep overnight in a warm place in winter or a cool place in summer, but not in the refrigerator, for the dough to rise.

- In the morning knead dough again and divide into 6 balls.

- Clean the underside of a tava or griddle and place on heat upside down.

- Press a ball of dough flat. Slap the dough from one hand to the other and make a thick circular roti.

- Slap it on to the griddle and cook on both sides until bubbles are formed on the surface and they turn brown.

- Spread a little butter on it and keep wrapped in a closed box.

MAKKI KI ROTI

Cornmeal Roti

Makes: 4 roti

2 cups cornmeal (makki ka atta)
½ tsp salt
4 tbsp butter

- Mix salt and cornmeal together. Add ¼ cup hot water and mix with your fingers.

- Roll it with your hand on a flat surface, adding additional water, if necessary, to form a stiff dough.

- Divide dough into 4 portions. Sprinkle a little warm water over one portion and shape into a ball. Slap ball from one palm to the other to make a flat and thick roti ½-¾ cm thick. You could also place a cheese cloth on a flat surface, put the ball of dough on it, press down and rotate to form the roti.

- Place roti on a heated tava or griddle. Cook for 2 minutes over medium heat. With a flat spatula turn it over. Spread ¼ tablespoon butter on top and turn it over after 2 minutes. Spread butter over roti again, and rotate it on the griddle. Trickle ¼ tablespoon butter along the sides of the roti, cook for one minute more, turn over and repeat.

- The roti will have brown spots on both sides.

- Make each roti in the same way and serve hot with sarson da saag (p. 50).

Rice

MURGH BIRYANI
Chicken Biryani
Serves: 6

1 chicken, cut into serving pieces
½ cup oil
2 onions, finely chopped
1 tsp salt
2 cups basmati rice, washed and soaked in water for 1 hour
¾ cup curd, beaten till smooth
4 green chillies, chopped
1½ tsp garam masala powder
½ tsp saffron soaked in hot water

Ground to a paste for marinade:
2 tsp grated fresh ginger
2 tsp chopped garlic
2 onions, chopped
1 tsp salt

- Mix chicken with marinade and marinate for one hour.
- Heat oil in a pan and fry onions till golden.
- Add chicken and sauté for 5 minutes, until chicken is browned, sprinkling water if necessary and set aside.

- In another pan add 5 cups water and salt and bring to boil. Drain rice and add.

- Cook until rice is still firm and not completely done. When crushed between the fingers, it should feel as though it has a grain inside. Remove from heat and drain.

- Add curd, green chillies and garam masala to chicken and mix together. Stir in cooked rice and saffron.

- Cover pan and cook on low heat for 5 minutes. Place pan on a griddle and cook for a further 5 minutes.

- Serve biryani hot with salad and curd or any raita of your choice.

MUTTON BIRYANI

Serves: 6

500 gms mutton with bone, cut into serving pieces
1 tbsp oil
2 onions, finely sliced
¼ tsp powdered nutmeg
½ tsp garam masala powder
½ cup curd, beaten till smooth
1 tsp cumin seeds
4 cloves
20 black peppercorns
2 bay leaves (tej patta)
6 dry red chillies
3-cm stick cinnamon
3 black cardamoms, crushed
2 cups basmati rice, washed and soaked in water for 1 hour
3 tbsp ghee

Ground together for marinade:
1 tsp finely chopped raw papaya
2 tsp grated fresh ginger
3 tsp garlic paste

· Rub marinade into meat and allow to marinate for one hour.

· Heat oil in a pressure cooker and sauté onions till golden brown. Remove half the onions, drain and set aside.

· Add meat to cooker, sprinkle with nutmeg and garam masala powder, and sauté meat for 5 minutes. Add curd and mix well.

- Mix in ½ cup water and cook under pressure for 20 minutes. Cool and transfer to another pan. Sprinkle over reserved fried onions.

- In another pan add 5 cups water and whole spices and bring to boil. Drain rice and add. Remove from heat when rice is still firm and not completely done. When crushed between the fingers, it should feel as though it has a grain inside.

- Drain rice, place over the meat and dribble in melted ghee. Wrap a napkin over the pan and cover with a tight-fitting lid. Place on medium heat for 5 minutes. Lower heat, place a griddle under the pan and cook for 8-10 minutes further.

- Serve with lachedar onions, salad and any raita of your choice.

YAKHANI PULAO

Mutton or Chicken Pulao

Serves: 4

This is a light pulao and can be served during the summer and monsoon. People with a delicate stomach can avoid the meat but can eat the rice enriched with the meat flavour and the strengthening yakhani.

500 gms mutton with bone *or* chicken, cut into serving pieces
5 black peppercorns
1 bay leaf (tej patta)
6 cloves
1 black cardamom
½ tsp cumin seeds
1 tsp salt
1 cup basmati rice, washed and soaked in water for 1 hour

- Place all ingredients except rice in a pressure cooker with 3 cups water. Cook for 30 minutes if using mutton and 10 minutes if using chicken. Cool.

- Strain to separate meat and soup.

- Boil soup and add drained rice. Cook until rice is still firm and not completely done. When crushed between the fingers, it should feel as though it has a grain inside.

- Spread meat over rice. Cover pan and cook on low heat for 5-7 minutes.

- Serve hot with a dry vegetable dish and curd.

SABZI POLOW

Mutton and Herb Pulao from Iran

Serves: 6-8

Sabzi polow is made during spring in Iran when greens are available in plenty. It is also made for their Nourouz feast and is served with fish. I find that it can be served throughout the year.

1 kg mixed green vegetables like spring onions, fresh parsley, dill and coriander leaves
750 gms mutton, lamb *or* veal, cut into serving pieces
1 onion, chopped
Salt as required
1 kg basmati rice, washed and soaked in water for 1 hour.
2 tbsp oil
3 potatoes, peeled and cut into round slices
2 tbsp butter
½ tsp saffron soaked in water

- Wash and clean the greens leaf by leaf. Chop fine and mix together.

- Cook meat with 2 cups water, onion and one teaspoon salt in a pressure cooker for 30 minutes. Strain to separate meat and stock.

- Drain rice and cook in boiling salted water till done.

- Coat base of a large non-stick pan with oil. Line pan with potatoes. Lightly spread a layer of cooked rice over potatoes. Sprinkle a handful of chopped greens over rice. Continue with another layer of rice and remaining greens. Place the cooked meat in the centre of pan. Cover with remaining rice.

- Cover pan and place on medium heat for 10 minutes. Adjust heat to very low and cook for 10 minutes more.

- Make 4 holes in the rice, add butter into holes, cover pan and cook for a further 20 minutes.

- When ready to serve remove some rice from pan, mix with saffron and set aside. Remove meat from pan and set aside.

- Place rice and greens on a large platter. Sprinkle with saffron flavoured rice and place meat in the centre.

- Scrape out the crisp potatoes from bottom of pan and decorate pulao with them.

- Serve hot with any khoreshth—Iranian dish of vegetables and chicken or meat—of your choice.

TAH CHIN

Baked Rice and Lamb Pulao from Iran

Serves: 8

4 cups basmati rice, washed and soaked in water for 1 hour
Salt as required
3 tbsp oil
1 kg boneless lamb, cut into cubes
1 large onion, chopped
1-2 tomatoes, chopped
Pepper to taste
Extra oil for coating casserole

Mixed to a smooth paste:
2 cups curd, beaten till smooth
2 eggs
¼ tsp saffron
3 tbsp oil

- Cook rice till done, in boiling salted water. Drain, rinse with cool water and set aside.

- Heat oil in a pressure cooker and sauté meat till brown.

- Add onion and sauté for a few minutes longer.

- Add tomatoes and enough water to cover meat. Sprinkle in salt and pepper. Cook under pressure for 30 minutes.

- In a separate pan, mix a little more than half the rice with the curd mixture.

- Oil generously, a large flat casserole. Put in a layer of rice and curd mixture, and place meat and gravy over rice. Cover with plain rice. Top with remaining rice and curd mixture and pat down lightly.

- Place in an oven heated to 200°C (400°F) for approximately one hour. A beautifully golden crust should be formed at the base.

- Invert casserole on to a serving dish and serve immediately with crust-side up.

MEGHU POLOW BA TEH DEEG

Prawn Pulao with a Crust

Serves: 6-8

6 tbsp oil

2 cups shelled prawns, deveined and washed

Tamarind paste made from 1 rounded tsp tamarind soaked in 2 tbsp water *or* ½ tsp tamarind concentrate

3 tsp salt *or* to taste

3 medium-sized onions, finely chopped

½ cup finely chopped fresh coriander leaves

2 green chillies, finely chopped

2 medium-sized tomatoes, skinned and finely chopped

3 cups chicken stock *or* 3 chicken soup cubes dissolved in 3 cups hot water

1 tbsp tomato ketchup

2 cups basmati rice, washed and soaked in water for 1 hour

2 tbsp butter + extra butter for coating casserole

2 tbsp curd

Ground to a paste:

4 dry red chillies

6 cloves garlic

1 tsp cumin seeds

· Heat one tablespoon oil in a pan and fry ground paste for one minute. Add a little water if paste tends to stick to pan. Add prawns, fry for 2 minutes and set aside.

· Mix tamarind paste, one cup water and 2 teaspoons salt in a pan and cook on medium heat for 5 minutes.

- In another pan, heat 5 tablespoons oil and fry onions till light brown. Add coriander leaves, green chillies and tomatoes, cook for 3 minutes and add prawns. Simmer together for 2 minutes.

- Mix chicken stock with tomato ketchup in a large pan, bring to boil, drain rice and add one teaspoon salt. Cook rice till water is absorbed. Remove pan from heat.

- Rub butter over the base of a non-stick casserole with lid and coat with curd.

- Ladle in one-third of the rice, level it and spread half the prawns over the rice. Cover prawns with another one-third portion of rice and spread remaining prawns over it. Cover with remaining rice.

- Wrap lid with a cloth napkin and cover pan firmly. Lower heat to minimum and cook for 10 minutes.

- Open pan, make 5 holes in the rice, add one teaspoon butter in each hole and cover pan tightly again.

- Place on low heat and cook for another 10 minutes. Place on a griddle and keep it cooking for 20 minutes longer.

- Remove from heat when people are seated at the table. Invert a serving dish over the pan and turn pan. The rice will come out like a cake with a beautiful crust.

- Bring to the table and serve with the crust-side up.

Variation: **Herb Pulao with a Crust**
Replace prawns with diced carrots, French beans, spring onions and potatoes and chicken stock with water or a vegetable stock.

HARÉ CHANÉ PULAO
Fresh Green Gram Pulao

Serves: 4

This is ideal for spring and early summer when green gram is in season. I generally freeze the gram in 100-gm packets and use it for making a pulao later during the summer and monsoon seasons.

2 tbsp ghee
1 onion, sliced
3 green chillies, chopped
½ cup fresh green gram (hara chana), boiled
1 tsp salt
3 cloves
6 green cardamoms
2 bay leaves (tej patta)
3-cm stick cinnamon
1 tsp cumin seeds
½ cup basmati rice, washed and soaked in water for 1 hour
1 tbsp oil
¼ tsp saffron mixed with 2 tbsp curd, soaked and ground in a mortar and pestle
2 tbsp butter

Mixed together:

1½ tsp fresh ginger paste
1½ tsp garlic paste
1½ tsp onion paste

- Heat ghee in a pan and fry sliced onion till brown. Set aside half of the fried onion.

- Add ginger, garlic and onion paste to pan with green chillies and sauté for 2 minutes.

- Add boiled gram and sauté for 2 minutes. Mix in salt and remove from heat.

- In another pan put in 3 cups water, whole spices and cumin seeds, and bring water to boil. Add drained rice and cook till done. If any water is left, drain rice. Rinse rice in cold water and drain. Mix rice with gram.

- Coat sides and base of a non-stick pan with oil. Pour rice into pan in a cone-shaped heap. Pour in curd and saffron and spread out rice in pan. Make 4 holes in the rice and put butter into the holes.

- Cover pan and leave on low heat for another 5 minutes. Serve hot with the reserved fried onions sprinkled on top.

KHUSHBUDAR KHICHDI

Fragrant Khichdi

Serves: 6

Khichdi is the favourite food in Bengal during the rainy season. A range of khichdi is made by the Bengali housewife. It is light and easy to digest.

4 tbsp oil *or* ghee
2 medium-sized onions, finely sliced
1 tsp turmeric powder
1½ tsp coriander powder
½ tsp cumin powder
½ tsp cumin seeds
4 cloves
4-cm stick cinnamon
1 tsp whole green cardamoms, slit open
2 bay leaves (tej patta)
1 cup basmati rice, washed and soaked in water for 1 hour
⅓ cup husked Egyptian lentils (masoor dal), washed and soaked in water for 1 hour
1 tsp salt
10 drops kewra essence

- Heat oil in a pan and fry onions till brown. Remove half the onions and keep aside.

- Add all the spices and stir-fry for one minute.

- Drain water from rice and dal. Rinse dal in fresh water and add to pan with rice. Stir together and add 2½ cups water and salt. Bring to boil, lower heat and cook, partially covered, for 10 minutes.

- Cover pan completely and cook until rice and dal are tender.

- Add kewra essence and mix.

- Sprinkle with reserved fried onions and serve hot with crisp papad, fried vegetables, fried fish or fried Bombay duck, a salad and curd.

PANEER VALI KHICHDI
Khichdi with Cottage Cheese

Serves: 6

4 tbsp butter
3 onions, finely sliced
3-cm stick cinnamon
4 cloves
2 black cardamoms
1 tbsp black peppercorns
½ tsp turmeric powder
1 cup husked green beans (moong dal), washed and soaked in water
for ½ hour
1 cup basmati rice, washed and soaked in water for ½ hour
Salt to taste
200 gms cottage cheese (paneer), chopped into small pieces

- Heat 2 tablespoons butter in a pan and sauté onions until golden. Add whole spices and turmeric and sauté for one minute.

- Drain dal, rinse out in fresh water, add to pan and sauté for one minute.

- Add drained rice and sauté for a further minute. Pour in 3½ cups hot water, mix in salt and stir together.

- Bring to boil, cover pan and lower heat so that the rice cooks at a simmer.

- After 10 minutes, check rice. If it is three quarters done, make 4 holes in it and add remaining butter into the holes. Cover pan and cook till rice and dal are done.

- Gently stir in paneer, cook for a few minutes longer and serve hot.

Cooking for All Seasons

Variation: **Andé vali Khichdi (Khichdi with Eggs)**
Replace cottage cheese with:

> 8 eggs, beaten till frothy
> Salt and pepper to taste
> ½ cup fresh coriander leaves

- Cook khichdi as given above, but do not add butter to it. When cooked through remove from heat.

- Melt butter in a non-stick pan and rotate to cover base and sides. Place on low heat, put in one-third of the rice, spread gently and smoothen the surface. Mix together eggs, salt, pepper and coriander leaves. Spread half the egg mixture over the rice, cover pan and cook for 5 minutes till eggs are set.

- Spread another one-third portion of rice over eggs, smoothen the surface and pour over remaining egg mixture. Cover pan and allow the eggs to set. Add remaining rice and cover pan. Cook for 2 minutes. Make 4 holes in the rice and pour 2 tablespoons butter into them. Cover pan. Cook for another 6-8 minutes. Lower heat and cook for 5 minutes further.

- Remove from heat. Invert a large round serving dish over the pan, turn pan upside down, tap bottom and sides and gently lift up the pan.

- Serve immediately.

Sauces, Chutneys & Dips

SPICY DRESSING

Makes: 1 cup

2 tbsp flour
1 cup water
½ cup malt vinegar
¼ cup catsup *or* tomato ketchup
½ tsp powdered paprika
A pinch of pepper
1 tsp mustard powder
½ tsp Worcestershire sauce
A pinch of salt
1 clove garlic, peeled

- Mix flour and water in a small pan. Place on heat and boil for one minute.

- Cool and blend in remaining ingredients except garlic.

- Place in a jar, add garlic and refrigerate. Shake well before use.

DIET SALAD DRESSING

Makes: ¾ cup

½ cup tomato juice
2 tbsp lime juice *or* malt vinegar
1 tbsp finely chopped onion
Salt and pepper to taste

· Combine all ingredients and chill. Shake well before using.

Note: Chopped parsley, green bell pepper, dry mustard or horseradish may be added.

VINAIGRETTE DRESSING

Makes: about ½ cup

½ tsp salt
¼ tsp pepper
¼ tsp mustard powder
5 tbsp olive oil, corn oil *or* sunflower oil
2 tbsp malt vinegar *or* lime juice

· Mix dry ingredients with one tablespoon oil to a smooth paste in a screw-top jar.
· Add remaining ingredients, close jar and shake vigorously.
· Use immediately or store in a cool place.

BÉCHAMEL SAUCE

Makes: 2 cups

2 tbsp butter
2 tbsp flour
1 tsp salt
½ tsp white pepper powder
A pinch of grated nutmeg
2½ cups hot milk

· In a small saucepan, melt butter over medium heat. Stir in flour and cook. Do not allow it to colour.

· Add salt, pepper and nutmeg and stir in milk. Cook, stirring constantly, for 15 minutes.

Note: Béchamel sauce may be prepared in advance and stored in a refrigerator for several days.

Variation: **Sauce Mornay**
Five minutes before end of cooking, stir in 2 tablespoons grated Swiss cheese.

ZERO CALORIE SEAFOOD COCKTAIL SAUCE

Makes: 1 cup

½ cup tomato juice
1 tsp lime *or* lemon juice
½ tsp Worcestershire sauce
½ tsp salt
½ tsp finely chopped fresh parsley

· Combine all ingredients and chill.

GARDIANNE SAUCE

Makes: about 2 cups

2 cups mayonnaise
2 tbsp tomato paste
2 cloves garlic, crushed
½ tsp pastis *or* Ricardo (Anis aperitif)

· Mix all ingredients together. Taste and season as necessary.

SAUCE MOUTARDE

Makes: ¾ cup

1 tbsp butter *or* margarine
1 tbsp mustard powder
5 tbsp milk
Salt and pepper to taste

· Melt butter over low heat in a small pan. Add mustard and stir vigorously with a fork or wooden spoon to mix thoroughly.

· Add milk gradually and salt and pepper, and keep stirring until hot. Do not allow to boil.

· Serve immediately with any meat, fowl or vegetable dish.

SAUCE RAVIGOTE

Makes: 1 cup

2 hard-boiled eggs, separated
Juice of 1 lime
2 tbsp fresh herbs like parsley, mint, coriander etc., finely chopped
Salt and pepper to taste
½ cup oil

· Mash egg yolks with lime juice, herbs, salt and pepper. Discard egg whites.

· Add oil drop by drop and keep stirring.

· Serve with fish or you can even mix it with pasta.

AMB JHOL

Green Mango Chutney with a Light Gravy

Serves: 4-6

2 large *or* 4 medium-sized raw mangoes (about 400 gms)
¼ tsp turmeric paste, made by mixing turmeric powder with a little
water
1 tsp mustard oil
A pinch of panch poran (Bengal 5-spice mixture)
3-4 cups water
1 tsp salt
2 tbsp sugar *or* 3 tbsp grated jaggery

· Peel and cut mangoes into narrow strips lengthwise. Mix in turmeric paste.

· Heat oil in a kadhai or deep frying pan and when it is really hot, add panch poran. When it stops spluttering, lower heat, add mango slices and fry lightly for a couple of minutes.

· Pour in water. Add salt and sugar or jaggery and stir until sugar or jaggery melts. Simmer gently until mangoes are soft but not pulpy. Remove from heat and cool.

Note: Aam jhol should taste sweet and sour and have a large quantity of gravy. It is delightful when served in cups at the end of a meal. It is served as cold as possible. After a rich afternoon meal, sipping the thin syrupy gravy and biting on the soft mango slices will act as a remarkably cool digestive.

MANGO CHUTNEY

Serves: 6-8

6 large raw mangoes (about 1½ kg)
Salt for rubbing into mangoes
2 cups sugar

Ground to a paste:

6 dry red chillies
5-cm piece fresh ginger
2 cloves garlic
3 tbsp malt vinegar
Salt to taste

- Peel mangoes and cut lengthwise into thin slices. Rub with a little salt and keep aside.

- Heat 8 cups water in a large pan and add sugar. Stir till dissolved and bring to boil removing any scum that may appear. Lower heat and continue simmering for about 10 minutes.

- Add ground paste and simmer for 5 minutes longer.

- Add mangoes and continue simmering until syrup thickens and mangoes are cooked.

- Cool and serve at room temperature at the end of a meal.

PAPAYA CHUTNEY

Serves: 4

250 gms raw papaya, peeled and sliced into juliennes
A walnut-sized ball of tamarind without seeds and fibre, soaked in ½
cup water
1 tbsp sultanas (kishmish), cleaned, washed, soaked in water for
½ hour and dried
1 cup sugar
Salt to taste
1 tbsp dry mango powder (amchur)
1 tsp dry ginger powder (saunth)

Tempering:

2 tsp mustard oil
½ tsp mustard seeds
3-4 dry whole red chillies, broken in half

- Soak papaya in water for 30 minutes and drain. Boil in 1½ cups water for 5 minutes. Drain and dry with a towel.

- Heat oil for tempering in a kadhai or deep frying pan over high heat, till a blue haze appears over the oil.

- Add mustard seeds and chillies. When they start sputtering, add papaya. Cook over high heat until water given out by papaya is absorbed.

- Extract tamarind paste and add with sultanas, sugar and salt. Simmer over medium heat until gravy thickens. Mix in dry mango and ginger. Adjust salt and simmer for 5 minutes.

- Serve either hot or at room temperature.

COCONUT CHUTNEY

Makes: 1 cup

1 tbsp oil
¼ tsp powdered asafoetida (hing)
3 tbsp Bengal gram (chana dal), cleaned, washed and drained
4 dry red chillies, broken into small pieces
¾ cup grated fresh coconut *or* 8 tbsp dry coconut

Tempering:

2 tsp oil
1 tsp mustard seeds
10 curry leaves
1 dry red chilli

- Heat oil and add asafoetida. Stir for ½ minute. Add dal and sauté for a few moments. Add red chillies and fry for a few seconds. Stir in coconut and sauté for one minute.

- Remove from heat. Cool. Blend together in a food processor with a little water and put into a serving bowl.

- In the same pan heat oil for tempering, add mustard seeds, curry leaves and red chilli and stir. When mustard seeds sputter, pour over chutney and mix.

D O ' A

Egyptian Snack Powder

Makes: 1 cup

This Egyptian snack powder is similar to the Tamilian podi, which can be eaten with pita bread dipped in oil. Mixed into a paste, it can be spread on a chapatti or bread.

50 gms sesame seeds (til)
25 gms coriander seeds
25 gms cumin seeds
2 whole dry red chillies (optional)
Salt to taste

- Clean the seeds very well, removing all small stones, and wash them. Spread them out to dry.

- Gently roast each ingredient except salt, separately in a frying pan, shaking them in the pan to avoid burning.

- The sesame seeds should become golden in colour but not dark brown, as that will make it bitter. The other ingredients should be roasted for 3-4 minutes each.

- Grind all together. The colour should be light to medium-brown. Mix in salt and store in an airtight container.

- Serve as a dip with drinks or as a snack at any time.

Note: The original recipe does not contain red chillies. I add them as they give an extra flavour.

ELLU PODI

Sesame Seed Powder

Makes: 1 cup

In the Deccan, they make delicious dry powders, which can be added to plain hot rice with ghee or butter, or spread on toast, or used to convert a boring dish into one full of aroma and taste. I always keep some in my refrigerator and they are very easy to make. In Tamil Nadu they are called podi.

1 tbsp oil
¼ tsp powdered asafoetida (hing)
½ cup sesame seeds (til)
3 tbsp dry grated coconut
6 dry red chillies
1 tsp salt

- Heat oil in a pan and add asafoetida. Sauté for half minute. Add sesame seeds and sauté for one minute.

- Add coconut and red chillies and sauté for a minute further.

- Remove from heat and add salt.

- Cool and blend to a powder.

- Store in an airtight container.

THENGAI PODI

Coconut Powder

Makes: 1 cup

½ fresh coconut, grated
2 tbsp pigeon peas (toover or arhar), washed and drained
2 tbsp Bengal gram (chana dal), washed and drained
1 tsp oil
¼ tsp powdered asafoetida (hing)
6 dry red chillies, broken into pieces
½ tsp salt

- In a dry pan roast grated coconut till golden. Remove from pan and set aside.

- Add the dals to the same pan and roast for 3 minutes. Remove from pan and set aside.

- Add oil to the same pan and fry asafoetida for half minute. Add red chillies and fry for a few seconds.

- Blend together to a powder and mix in salt.

- Store in an airtight container.

KARIVEPILAI PODI

Curry Leaf Powder

Makes: 1½ cups

1 bunch curry leaves (40-50 leaves)
2 tsp oil
½ cup coriander seeds
1 tbsp black peppercorns
1 tbsp cumin seeds
1 tbsp Bengal gram (chana dal)
1 tbsp whole black beans (sabut urad)
¼ tsp fenugreek seeds (methi)
2 tbsp crushed jaggery
1 tbsp dry mango powder (amchur)
1 tsp salt

- Dry roast curry leaves and set aside.

- Heat a little oil at a time in a pan and roast each of the remaining ingredients except jaggery, mango powder and salt.

- Mix all ingredients, grind and store in an airtight container.

Table of Measures

The cup measure used in this book is an 8-oz cup
(225 ml)

1 tsp = 5 ml
1 tbsp = 3 tsp
A pinch = ⅛ tsp (literally a pinch)
A dash = 1-2 drops

All spoon measures are level

List of Ingredients

Allspice   Kabab cheeni
Almond   Badam
Amaranth   Cholai bhaji
Aniseed   Saunf
Apple   Seb
Apricot   Khurmani / zardaloo /
        jerdaloo
Asafoetida   Hing
Ash gourd   Petha
Aubergine   Baingan
Baking soda   Meetha soda
Bamboo shoot Baans ki kalli
Banana   Kela
–green   Kaccha kela
Bay leaf   Tej patta
Beef   Gai ka gosht
Beetroot   Chukunder
Bell pepper / capsicum Shimla mirch
Bengal gram
–flour   Besan
–green   Hara chana
–husked   Chana dal
–roasted   Bhuné chané
–whole   Kala chana

Bitter gourd	Karela
Black beans	
–whole	Sabut urad
–husked	Urad dal
Black cumin seeds	Kala jeera / shahi jeera
Black pepper	Kali mirch
Black pomfret	Halva
Bombay duck	Sooka boomla
Bottle gourd	Ghia / lauki
Brain	Magaz / bheja
Butter	Makkhan
–clarified	Ghee
Cabbage	Band gobhi
Caraway seeds	Shahi jeera / kala jeera
Cardamom	
–black	Badi elaichi
–green	Hari elaichi / chhoti elaichi
Carrot	Gaajar
Cashewnut	Kaju
Cauliflower	Phool gobhi
Chicken	Murgh
Chickpeas	Kabuli channa / safaid channa
Chilli	Mirchi
–dried red	Sookhi mirch
–green	Hari mirch
–red	Lal mirch
Cinnamon	Dalchini
Cloves	Laung
Coconut	
–dry	Kopra
–fresh	Nariyal
–milk	Nariyal ka doodh
Colocasia	Arvi
Coriander	
–fresh	Hara dhania
–seeds	Sabut dhania

List of Ingredients

Corn	Makkai
–meal	Makki ka atta
Cottage cheese	Paneer
Cream	Malai
Cucumber	Kheera / kakdi
Cumin seeds	Jeera
Curd	Dahi
Curry leaf	Kari patta
Date	Khajoor
Dill	Sua saag
Drumsticks	Surjan ki phalli
Duck	Badak
Egg	Anda
Egyptian lentils	
–husked	Masoor dal
–whole	Sabut masoor
Fennel seeds	Badi saunf
Fenugreek	
–dry leaves	Kasuri methi
–fresh leaves	Methi saag
–seeds	Methi dana
Fig	Anjeer
Fish	Machchi / Machchli
French beans	Fransbin
Garlic	Lasun
Ginger	
–dry	Saunth
–fresh	Adrak
Grapes	Angoor
Green beans	
–husked	Moong dal
–whole	Sabut moong
Green peas	Mattar
Honey	Madh / Shahad
Horse radish	Safaid mooli
Indian hog plum	Amla
Indian squash	Tinda

Indian sour plum	Kokum
Jack fruit	Kathal
Jaggery	Gurd
Kidney beans	Rajma
Kingfish / seer	Surmai
Kohlrabi	Ganth gobhi
Leeks	Vilaiti pyaz
Lime	Limbu / nimbu
Liver	Kaleji
Mango	Aam
–dry powder	Amchur
Marrow	Ghia / lauki
Milk	Doodh
–dry unsweetened	Khoya
Mince	Keema
Mint	Pudina
Mulberry	Shahtoot
Mushroom	Dhingri / khumi
Mustard	
–greens	Sarson ka saag
–oil	Sarson ka tel
–seeds	Sarson / rai
Mutton	Gosht
Nutmeg	Jaiphal
Okra	Bhindi
Onion	Pyaz
Onion seeds	Kalaunji
Orange	Santra / narangi
Palm sugar	Tardh gurd
Papaya	Papeeta
–raw	Kaccha papeeta
Parsley	Ajmod
Peach	Aadu
Peanut	Mungphali
Peppercorn	Kali mirch
Pigeon peas	Arhar / toover dal
Pistachio nuts	Pista

Pomegranate	Anar
—seeds	Anardana
Pomfret	Chhamna / paplet
Poppy seeds	Khus khus
Pork	Suvar ka gosht
Potato	Alu
Prawn	Jhinga
Pumpkin	
—red / yellow	Seetaphul / kaddu
Radish	
—white	Safaid mooli
Raisin	Munakka
Rice	Chaval
Rose water	Gulabjal
Saffron	Kesar / Zafran
Sago	Sabudana
Salt	Namak
Sardines	Tarli
Screwpine flower essence	Kewra
Semolina	Sooji / Rava
Sesame	Til
Shrimp	Jhinga / kolmi
Spinach	Palak
Spring onions	Hara pyaz
Sugar	Cheeni / shakkar
Sultana	Kishmish
Tamarind	Imli
Tomato	Tamatar
Turmeric	Haldi
Turnip	Shalgam
Vermicelli	Sevian
Vinegar	Sirka
Walnut	Akhroat
Water melon	Tarbooz
Wheat	Gehun

Wheat	
–plain / refined flour	Maida
–whole wheat flour	Atta
Yam	Zimikand
Yoghurt	Substitute for dahi /curd

Note:

Ajwain — An umbelliferous plant which grows in India and the Far East. It is sometimes referred to as carom seeds and belongs to the same family as the Ethiopian bishop's weed and English lovage.

Bathua — The botanical name for bathua is *Chenopodium album*. It is a kind of cress, which is readily available during the winter and spring months in India, where other leafy green vegetables like mustard greens are sold.

Panch poran — A Bengali spice mixture made with five whole spices—onion seeds, aniseed, fenugreek seeds, mustard seeds and coriander seeds.

Basil, Broccolili, Capers, Chives, Fennel bulb, Haricot beans, Lemon grass, Oregano, Snow peas, Zucchini — These ingredients have no Indian names but are readily available in speciality shops.

Bean curd, Cloud-ear fungus, Chilli-hot oriental sesame oil, Dark soya sauce, Fun sie (cellophane noodles), Lemu omani (dried lemon), Nam pla (fish oil), Oriental peanut oil, Oriental sesame oil, Oyster sauce, Sweet thick soya sauce

These items are readily available in stores that stock Chinese and other oriental foodstuff.

I n d e x

Kway swe (Burmese chicken curry with noodles) 183
Murgh chana (chicken with chickpeas) 84
Murgh palak methi taridar (chicken curry with fenugreek and
    spinach) 154
Rice-noodles and nonya sauce with coconut 181

CHUTNEYS
Amb jhol (green mango chutney with a light gravy) 237
Coconut chutney 240
Mango chutney 238
Papaya chutney 239

DRESSINGS
Diet salad dressing 233
Spicy dressing 232
Vinaigrette dressing 233

DIPS
Do'a (Egyptian snack powder) 241
Ellu podi (sesame seed powder) 242
Karivepilai podi (curry leaf powder) 244
Thengai podi (coconut powder) 243

DUCK
Fesenjan (chicken or duck in pomegranate sauce) 39

EGGS
Egg curry with coconut 42

FISH
Bombay duck and aubergine curry 156
Dried fish and tomato curry 189
Fish molee 40
Isso baydun (Sri Lankan prawn curry) 90

Yakhani pulao (mutton or chicken pulao) 219

Vegetarian:
Haré chané pulao (fresh green gram pulao) 226
Herb pulao with a crust 225
Khushbudar khichdi (fragrant khichdi) 228
Paneer vali khichdi (khichdi with cottage cheese) 230

SALADS
Non-vegetarian:
Avocado puree with tuna 137
Chicken and almond salad 132·
Cold chicken salad 131
Potato and egg salad 129
Rice salad 97
Salade nicoise 136
Summer harlequin salad 133
Sweet and sour summer salad 130
Vietnamese salad 134

Vegetarian:
Bottle gourd salad 175
Burmese papaya salad 43
Crudité basket with three dips 127
Cucumber salad – Moscow style 125
Mixed bean salad 96
Pumpkin salad 176
Sesame and green bean salad 126
Spinach and cheese salad 128

SAUCES
Béchamel sauce 234
Gardianne sauce 235
Sauce mornay 234
Sauce moutarde 236
Sauce ravigote 236

Zero calorie seafood cocktail sauce 235

Celery:
Savoury celery 34

Curd:
Bathua ka raita (spiced curd with greens) 95
Maji's fried curd 197
Pakodivali kadhi (curd sauce with gram flour dumplings) 158

Drumsticks:
Dohroo (sweet and sour drumsticks – Parsi style) 192
Surjan ke patté ki sabzi (fried drumstick leaves) 191

Green peas:
Matar paneer (Green peas with cottage cheese) 48

Green beans (moong):
Moong dal aur sua saag (husked green beans with dill) 49

Kohlrabi (ganth gobhi):
Ganth gobhi taridar (curried kohlrabi) 47

Jackfruit:
Kathal curry (curried green jackfruit) 160

Leafy greens:
Bathua ka raita (spiced curd with greens) 95
Haaq saag (savoury Kashmir greens) 194
Palak methi taridar (fenugreek with spinach) 155
Sarson da saag (puréed mustard greens) 50

Mixed vegetables:
Lightly spiced vegetable stew 44
Vegetable cutlets 52

Mushroom:
Bean curd with dried mushrooms 198
Mushroom pâté 177